SOMER[barcode] TALES OF M[barcode] AND MURDER

———— ❀ ————

Roger Evans

COUNTRYSIDE BOOKS
NEWBURY, BERKSHIRE

First published 2004
© Roger Evans 2004

COUNTRYSIDE BOOKS
3 Catherine Road
Newbury, Berkshire

To view our complete range of books,
please visit us at
www.countrysidebooks.co.uk

ISBN 1 85306 863 2

Designed by Mon Mohan

Produced through MRM Associates Ltd., Reading
Typeset by Jean Cussons Typesetting, Diss, Norfolk
Printed by J. W. Arrowsmith Ltd., Bristol

Contents

MAP OF SOMERSET

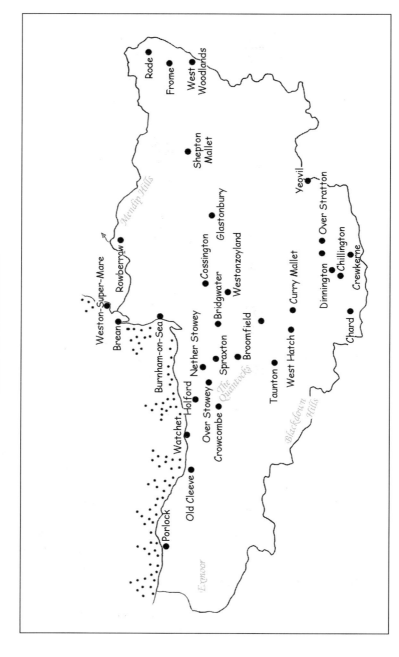

MYSTERY AT BREAN DOWN FORT

❁

Dominating the skyline along a considerable length of the Somerset coast, Brean Down stands proud from the sea as an extension of the Mendip Hills, reaching out towards the distant Welsh coastline. This mile-long, turf-down promontory, which was once an island, stands at just over 200 ft high. Used by the Romans as an enormous quay where ships could load under shelter, Brean Down nearly became a major port on the Atlantic in the mid 19th century and work actually started on the harbour. Unfortunately, the work was destroyed by a storm and the project was abandoned. But it is the history of the fort on Brean Down to which we draw our attention, for here was a military installation that was unexpectedly destroyed by a huge explosion in 1900. Destroyed at the same time was young Gunner Haines who became the scapegoat for this episode – but was he just an innocent victim?

The history of the fort takes us back to the 1860s when Britons lived in fear of a French invasion under the command of Emperor Napoleon III, who, the British suspected, was attempting to emulate, but with greater success, his great uncle, Napoleon Bonaparte. To guard against such attacks, the Prime Minister, Lord Palmerston, had a series of forts built around the English shores at enormous expense to the nation. In the Bristol Channel these were positioned at Lavernock Point on the coast of South Wales, on Flat Holme and Steep Holme in the channel, and at Brean Down on the English side. The strategic positioning of these forts with their gun emplacements would have made any attempted invasion in these waters extremely hazardous.

Fears of the invasion must have waned considerably, for it took several years to complete the project. Four acres of land were bought in 1862, work commenced on 21st December 1864, and the buildings were completed by 1870. The fort was situated 60 ft above sea level, at the end of the finger promontory of Brean Down, and reached by land along a military road built for the purpose. From the end of that road, access was gained by a bridge over a 12 ft dry moat. This provided a landward defence, the other side being defended by thick, high walls around the top of the steep cliffs.

Having crossed the bridge, to the left was the guardroom, with flat topped, limestone-walled quarters for the two NCOs and twenty men; to the right there was accommodation for four officers, plus the kitchen and scullery. Beyond that were buildings forming three sides of a small parade-ground area, and still further on were the sea-facing gun positions and magazines.

However, the guns were not positioned until 1877, by which time Napoleon III had fallen from power and with him the threat to our shores. And so the seven muzzle-loaded seven inch guns, each weighing seven tons and with a range of over half a mile, remained silent, other than during practice firing sessions, when the 1st Gloucestershire Volunteers went through their paces – that is, until 5 am on 6th July 1900, when the guns themselves came under attack from a totally unexpected quarter and two of them were blown to pieces.

Gunner Haines was one of the crew stationed at the fort. Described as conscientious and reliable, and a soldier of exemplary behaviour, he nonetheless enjoyed the occasional trip into Weston-super-Mare or Burnham-on-Sea just as any other young man would. On the night in question, he had been into Burnham, it is believed with a fellow soldier. Whether or not the outing had included a drink or two is not known but it would be a reasonable assumption. But how much had he drunk?

Certainly we know that he walked back to the barracks, a distance of several miles, and one theory is that his pushbike had a puncture. We also know that he stopped en route for a short while at Squires Gate, where he talked to Edith Millier, the daughter of the family who lived there. When asked later, she said that the young gunner appeared quite sober and behaved in a perfectly natural and friendly fashion. However, it seems that he returned to the barracks after the curfew hour, and was consequently put on a charge to be dealt with in the morning. To a soldier whose previous record was without fault, this must have come as a blow – but was it something he would take in his stride or was it sufficient to tip the balance of his mind? In truth we shall never know.

Of one thing we can be certain, however: at 5 o'clock in the morning an enormous explosion rocked the headland, a blast which could be heard miles away along the coast and across the channel. The magazine holding three tons of powder in one hundred and seventy two zinc cartridge cylinders blew up, destroying two of the gun positions on the western defences and taking with it a considerable part of the barracks and a section of the outer wall that separated the fort from the moat. Huge coping stones of a couple of hundredweight each were found 200 yards from the blast, with one of these landing just a couple of feet from the main sleeping area. Amazingly, none of those within was killed. Just one officer was severely wounded by flying glass and Gunner Haines had been killed in the explosion. Fortunately, those were the only casualties in what could have been a far worse disaster, the main magazine and shifting lobby having survived, as did the two expense magazines. The expense cartridge store was totally demolished, also the two artillery stores.

But who was to blame? And here I feel the media must take some blame for a probable miscarriage of justice. This was a period of Edwardian sensitivity and sensibility. The public learned of the events at Brean Down and some aspects of the detail shocked them. It appears the body of Gunner Haines had been found unclothed. What kind of activity had led to such circumstances? Surely the fault lay with the naked man. No sensible person would behave in such a depraved way. It must have been Gunner Haines who had caused the explosion, but why?

His visit to Burnham the previous evening was assumed to have led to his return to the barracks in a state of drunkenness. The reprimand for his late return was further assumed to have led to the balance of his mind being disturbed to the point of suicide. The verdict of the enquiry into the incident, which took place at the Wellington Hotel, now known as the Berrow Inn, was that Gunner Haines had taken his own life when he 'fired a carbine loaded with ball cartridge down the shaft of the ventilator (into expense magazine number 3) whilst in a state of temporary insanity'.

Personally, I find this version of events somewhat dubious. To the sensitivities of the Edwardian era, it helped to explain away a situation that on the face of it was anathema to their expectations of acceptable standards of behaviour. Gunner Haines was a sitting target, and it would have taken a brave judge or magistrate to favour any other explanation. A man who could cavort naked around a barracks could be capable of anything. But it was all too easy.

Let us examine aspects of the evidence once again. Gunner Haines took the trip to Burnham by pushbike and then walked home for at least the latter part of the long journey, suggesting that he had suffered a puncture. On arrival at Squires Gate, not too distant from Brean Down, he encountered Edith Millier. Conversation passed between them, and to the best of our knowledge their communication was polite and sensible, for Edith reported that he was not drunk and was just a normal young soldier on his way back to his barracks.

Then he arrived back late at his barracks. Perhaps the flat tyre was an excuse and not the real reason – but it isn't a flogging offence! A soldier whose behaviour had previously been described as exemplary might be disappointed with being put on a charge, but it's hardly going to make him suicidal. Haines had thirteen years' experience in the army and wasn't going to be rattled by such a trivial incident.

And then we come to the question of his naked body and this must surely be the single issue that made it so easy for all other accusing suggestions to be given credibility. Such behaviour pointed the finger inexorably at Gunner Haines. But what if his nakedness was not of his own volition? Since those days of over a hundred years ago, our awareness of the effects of bomb blasts has increased considerably. The bombing raids of the Second World War and the devastating effect of terrorist bombings around the world add to our knowledge. We now know that it is not uncommon for the bodies of innocent bomb victims to be devoid of any clothing. Dependent on what is being worn, the force of the blast can strip the body of all garments. Indeed, we now know that the body of Gunner Haines was found without its head, legs and left arm, such was the force of the explosion. Such details would have been suppressed in the prim Edwardian days.

What would have been the attitude of our Edwardian ancestors if Gunner Haines's body had been found fully clothed? Would there have been speculation as to his sobriety or drunkenness? Or would he have been hailed as the victim of a dreadful accident or of terrorist activity perhaps, in fact, an unsung hero? I suspect the latter. So let us make one assumption and one only and that is that his clothing was blasted from his body. An innocent visit to the latrines in his nightwear—bearing in mind that this was midsummer—would have left him vulnerable to the blast, of which he would have had no forewarning.

For simply being in the wrong place at the wrong time and the victim not just of the blast but of the prejudicial attention of press and public opinion, has Gunner Haines, previously respected, been unjustifiably slighted? And if so, where does the blame then lie? Just seven months before this incident, Irish Nationalist leader John Redmond called for an uprising against the British, and the following day General White repelled a fierce attack from the Boers at Ladysmith in South Africa. There were without doubt elements both at home and abroad only too willing to carry out a major coup – such as a stealthy attack on a military site – against the British forces on their home ground.

In focusing so readily on Gunner Haines, the alternative possibilities had been swept under the carpet at the expense of the soldier's reputation. Despite the conclusions of the enquiry, with a better understanding of the effects of bomb explosions we must now consider that there was almost certainly a different solution to this mystery.

Not-so-secret weapons

In the years that followed, the military moved out and the fort was used as a tearoom until the Second World War when it was chosen as the site for a Coast Artillery Battery. Many alterations were made to the Victorian structure, including the addition of two concrete gun houses for six inch ex-naval guns, two searchlights, plus various huts to house the garrison and provide the necessary facilities required to maintain a 20th-century gunnery position. Later in the war, when the threat of a German invasion had receded, the Directorate of Miscellaneous Weapons Development used the tip of Brean Down for weapons trials. And herein lay another series of mysteries. This remote headland was an ideal outpost for the secret activities of the Admiralty's research and development plans.

Brean is a fairly inaccessible place and the fort on the end of the down even more remote from prying eyes. I have heard Berrow described as the 'last place on earth that I would go and Brean can be found beyond that'. It's an unfair description, I hasten to add, other than in its geographic reference to the relative remoteness of the two communities. Across the bay to the north can be found Birnbeck Island at the top end of Weston-super-Mare, linked to the mainland by a pier. In 1882 the island was home to Weston's lifeboat station, but it was much later, in 1941, that the island was taken over by the Admiralty as HMS Birnbeck, to be used as another part of its top secret weapons research centre. Amongst the many weapons developed and tested both here and at Brean Down were torpedo decoys, the Expendable Noisemaker, the ship-launched anti-submarine missile AMUCK, and sea-borne versions of the Barnes Wallis bouncing bombs used so effectively against the dams providing power to Germany's industrial base.

Whilst strenuous attempts were made to keep everything under a cloak of complete secrecy, rumours broke out, and the locals could only speculate as to what was going on. Although most activity remained a total mystery, some aspects were brought to the public attention in the most dramatic way. One such example was during the trials of the Expendable Noisemaker. One of these devices was launched off the end of Brean Down, well away from prying eyes. It was supposed to work by emitting rhythmic detonations, thus attracting the attention of enemy submarines and their torpedoes. Unfortunately, the rocket that launched it off the end of the down made an unexpected turn and headed inland. At rapid speed it soon hit the seven-mile long beach and made for a Brean village farm. The explosion could be heard at the far end of the down, and those in charge of the experiment jumped into the vehicles and made a frantic descent to the village, where they discovered a farmer blackened from head to foot and in a state of concussed confusion.

'Whatever has happened?' they enquired of the luckless farmer. 'Buggered if I know,' he replied, 'but summat just blown up my chicken house!' 'Was there much damage?' asked the military. 'Cors there were,' came the response, 'I were innit at the time!'

Another disaster came with the trials of the sea-borne bouncing bombs. At the end of Brean Down one can still see what appears to be a short stretch of railway track going nowhere, just pointing out to sea. This formed part of the bouncing bomb experiment. The theory was that bombs could be bounced out to enemy ships just as they had successfully bounced in the famous Dam Busters Raid. The experimental bomb was placed on a trolley at one end of the track and then propelled at a tremendous speed until, on impact with the buffers at the track end, the trolley would stop and the bomb would launch itself seaward towards the enemy. Sadly it didn't quite work out that way. The impact of the combined weight of trolley and bomb was such that the buffers were ripped off and buffers, trolley and bomb plummeted over the cliff edge into the sea below.

In the year 2000, the National Trust bought the now dilapidated but historic old fort at the bargain price of £1 from Sedgemoor District Council and then began a project to restore it, in part at least, to its former glory.

The restored fort at Brean Down

THE BEAST OF EXMOOR

---✿---

Unresolved for decades, here is a mystery that runs and runs, just like the creature at the centre of the story. The beast, as it is known, could equally be called the Beast of Sedgemoor, the Blackdown Beast or the Mendip Beast, for it has been sighted in all of these areas. But let's start with Exmoor, which is a wild and beautiful expanse of over 260 square miles of National Park moorland straddling the Somerset and Devon border, the greater part lying within the county of Somerset. In the long cold winters, the winds and rains beat mercilessly across the open moor, providing a harsh environment for the hardy sheep that dominate it, sheep which, if we believe the beast exists, provide its staple diet. In summer, when the tourists abound – and perhaps such a creature would be easy to spot with so many visitors on the lookout for it – the bracken stands high and dense, offering ample cover for any lurking predator.

If large cats roam the moor, and I use cats in the plural very deliberately, they will not be restrained by political borders. They will cross from Somerset to Devon, unaware of the boundary, and, hence, in describing the events below, I likewise ignore those boundaries and include reports from Devon with those for Somerset.

In 1976 the Exotic Pets Act was introduced, which required owners of potentially dangerous exotic species of animals to apply for a licence to keep them and to register all animals kept. Their premises were also liable to inspection to ensure the chosen species could be safely contained. For some, perhaps irresponsible, owners this bureaucracy was undoubtedly a step too far or the cost of improving security too great, and hence a number of exotic animals were released into the wild, defeating the very purpose of the Act at least in the short term.

So here perhaps is one explanation as to how wild cats could be wandering the moors. Pumas, in particular, would be well suited to life in such conditions. There is no reason why this shy animal should not breed successfully in our countryside and remain unnoticed, well hidden in the undergrowth even during the tourist season when its cubs would require hunting activity to be at its peak. It would pose no threat to humans at any time and would do its utmost to avoid any such contact. Larger cats, such as lions, leopards and tigers, would be unlikely to survive and certainly unlikely to go unnoticed.

These days, grey squirrels run rife in our woodlands; wallabies, porcupines, coypu, mink, muntjac and sika deer are all now so well established that many of these are classified as pests—so is the prospect of pumas on Exmoor such a ridiculous idea?

The loss of ewes and lambs is an unwanted but expected event for sheep farmers on the hills of Exmoor. A percentage of the flock will always be lost each year. In part this comes from natural causes but also, an unfortunate fact of life, from kills by pet dogs allowed to roam free. Shepherds will normally shoot marauding dogs that are attacking their sheep, if they can catch them in the act. They are well used to finding the bodies of ewes and lambs killed in this fashion and are sufficiently accustomed to such kills as to be able to identify the likely cause of death by the way the body or carcass has been mutilated. Dogs attack by daylight as much as by night.

Across the border in Devon, one farmer in 1983 lost thirty sheep before spring was halfway through and, in each case, the attacks came by night – and just one sheep in each attack. Unusually, the remainder of the flock continued grazing, apparently unaware, which is not the case with dog attacks where the flock become visibly nervous. It was as if the attacker came unseen, killed, and disappeared undetected by the remainder of the flock. This was more akin to the behaviour pattern of the large cats. With the sheep's throat bitten through and the neck broken, it was something quite out of the ordinary.

Police and farmers combined to form a hunting party, aided by a pack of beagles and a police helicopter, but to no avail. With the publicity this generated, more people came forward with reported sightings, mostly describing a black panther-like animal. The incidence of attacks increased and, with the local publicity of the hunting parties, the national press picked up the story. A name was needed for the beast and the 'Beast of Exmoor' had arrived.

Almost certainly the beast was a puma, a particularly non-aggressive member of the cat family and, as such, a popular pet in the 1950s and 1960s; undoubtedly there were pumas released into the wild by irresponsible owners. However, despite the evidence pointing to a predator other than a dog, the official line remained that a dog was the culprit. A number of dogs roaming the moors were shot but still the problem remained. By the end of April 1983, the police requested the help of the Royal Marine Commandos based at Lympstone in Devon. Surely the Commandos wouldn't be called in if the authorities genuinely believed the predator was a dog!

The kills continued, with the carcasses stripped of the flesh and the evidence indicating that the sheep had broken necks and torn throats. The bodies were almost unbruised, indicating a quick kill in cat fashion, with minimal struggle – unlike a dog attack—and just one animal at a time. The Commandos arrived with a real challenge on their hands. The rules of engagement dictated that they could only fire if the animal to be destroyed was downhill from them, with solid ground behind it to entrap any stray bullet. It was also going to be difficult to operate should any members of the public be around. They set up their headquarters in a cattle shed and began the search. Operation Beastie had begun.

In the days that followed, the Marines went out on their daily and nightly patrols, doing their best to ignore the increasing media presence in what was now seen as a 'silly season' for the newshounds. Bed and breakfast premises, hotels and village stores were doing a booming trade. Apart from temporarily scaring the beast away, though, this media frenzy was making conditions impossible for the Marines to operate. There was too great a risk of a civilian injury and so the officer in charge provided the press with a briefing session, accompanied by Marines in camouflage for a photo call. This gave them all something to write about and hopefully would keep them out of the way for a few days to come.

During this time the official line remained that the predator was a dog. Cats were not to be mentioned. One Marine, having spotted the beast himself, initially described what he had seen through his rifle sights as a big black and powerful cat-like creature. However, within hours, his story had altered to having seen a dog-like creature. Under whose instructions had this change of description occurred and why was it so important not to mention a cat-like creature? And then all hell broke loose. A national paper offered a £1,000 reward for the capture of the beast and the Commandos soon realised the whole area could be overrun with gunmen, licensed and unlicensed, and there was no way they could operate under such conditions. Their services were withdrawn.

Weeks passed by until a period of torrential rain ensured that any potential bounty hunters lost interest and went home. The animal kills continued and, in time, the police requested the return of the Marines to finish the job they had previously started and had been obliged to abandon. Continued sightings were now suggesting that at least two animals were present and this fitted in with tracks found by the Marines, which showed one large animal and a smaller one running alongside, perhaps a cub. This also tallied with the reports of a large black cat-like creature about the size of a labrador and another described as about half that size and lighter in colour.

Various ploys were tried to lure the beasts into range of the snipers' fire. The carcass of a dead bullock was left to attract the predator but to no avail. Wherever the Marines lay in wait, the beast made its kill elsewhere as if it knew the plot. Eleven weeks of such activity passed by, with a number of dogs being shot, and with actual sightings of the beast by the Marines themselves, albeit with no successful shots to kill it. One attempted shot failed to hit its target; it was later realised the sights had been aligned for a different marksman. But the amazing thing in this case was the cat's reaction. Instead of quickly heading for cover, it turned to challenge its attacker until deterred by a second failed shot. Faced with failure, eventually the Marines withdrew.

In time, the press interest waned but the mystery killings still went on. The number of reported sightings diminished but to some extent only because sightings were so frequent that they no longer justified reporting. So is the beast still there? And, indeed, are there a number of beasts? In all probability, there are.

The animals described in these sightings fall into two categories: the large black and the smaller fawn coloured. The consistency of these descriptions is such that it strongly suggests more than one beast. And the number of years over which the sightings have been reported, which exceeds the normal life expectancy of wild cats, indicates that, if large cats they are, they either continue to be released or, and more likely in my opinion, they successfully breed in the remoter areas of our moors.

Somerset folklore is also full of tales of 'big black dog-like' creatures that haunt the moor. Hell hounds, devil dogs or however they are described, the stories all have the same basic theme. The poor unsuspecting traveller, whilst walking across the moor or through woodland, comes face to face with this terrifying creature. The size of a big black labrador or even larger, it is invariably described more as dog-like than as an actual dog. It screams rather than barks. Its eyes reflect back the light, like a cat rather than a dog. Its head is flat-faced and sunk back into the beast's shoulders – again more feline than canine. It bounds away more in the style of a leaping deer rather than a striding canine.

In those days of long ago, when country folk had such encounters, it is reasonable that their descriptions of what they saw should be based on their understanding of what the creature was most likely to be. They would draw on the animals with which they were familiar – and large cats would not be part of their experience. Hence, if they were to come across a large cat in their travels at least the size of a labrador, their account of the happening would have been based on the closest fit within their experience. It would be described as dog-like with a flat face on a head that sat well back into the shoulders. If it looked like a dog, it would be called a dog.

When we compare these mysterious sightings with those of more modern times, it begs the question: 'Have beasts such as these wandered Exmoor and the Somerset countryside for centuries or is this a new phenomenon?' These days, of course, descriptions of the beasts are based on a greater knowledge of the various members of the cat family, thanks to zoos, global travel and TV documentaries.

Sightings

The sightings continue but with far fewer being reported. In June 1991 a labrador-sized cat was seen near Watchet, described as some three feet in length and behaving in a very feline fashion in its movement and form. It was a sighting which Dr Gerald Legg,

Keeper of Biology at the Booth Museum in Brighton, described as meriting further examination.[1] On 7th August 1995 a man from Pawlett near Bridgwater filmed a large black cat in fields near his home which appeared to be some six feet in length and half that in height.

In December 1992 a large black cat was sighted three times in one week just to the north of Bridgwater. Susan Stretch and her neighbour Lynn Wardle were travelling at night in a car with five children on board. As they passed along a lane near the village of Cossington, they saw a big black creature with massive teeth whose head was as high as the windows of their Citroen car. Spotting the creature in the lane, well lit by her headlights, the driver braked to avoid a collision, at which point the cat attacked the car, crashing into its side hard enough for those within to believe it had killed itself – which, needless to say, it hadn't. The children in the back screamed, believing they were all about to be devoured until they realised the creature had left them alone.[2]

In the spring of 2000, in the Blackdown Hills, on a number of occasions, a puma was sighted which was described as around five feet long with a tail about half that length again and fawn in colour.[3] On one such occasion, nearby was the body of a full

[1] *Mammal Society News* No. 87
[2] *Evening Standard*, 16 December 1992
[3] *Western Daily Press*, 8 June 2000

grown roe deer. The lady who witnessed this went home to fetch her brother, by which time the carcass had been dragged away some distance and more of it consumed. Later still it was rediscovered at the entrance to a culvert where yet another deer carcass was found, perhaps suggesting the puma was taking the carcasses to where her cubs were holed up.

In the summer of 2000 my wife was crossing the Quantock Hills between Bridgwater and Taunton. As she passed along Buncombe Hill, a large animal came out through the woods and leapt in cat-like fashion from a high bank down into the road. Black in colour, feline in shape and in gait, it crossed the road in front of her car. In describing its size, she put its length at slightly greater than the width of the car, so about five feet long and about two and a half feet high. Pulling up in surprise, she found two other drivers had likewise stopped just behind her, both asking 'Did you see what I just saw?' and reassuring my wife that she was not hallucinating. This was definitely no dog, no horse and no deer.

August 2001 brought a number of reported sightings of a lioness near Churchill, described as big and tan in colour, but expert opinion was that it was almost certainly a puma that can easily be mistaken for a lioness to the untrained eye. Since pumas are not considered a risk to the public, that was the end of that story.[4]

In December 2001 a large pitch-black cat was sighted a number of times around Wellington and Milverton, with descriptions of its size ranging from three to six feet in length. The examination of a photograph of its paw prints, which showed no claw depressions as would be left by a dog, had a pad pattern closer to feline than canine and led an expert to state it was possibly a lynx.[5]

In the spring of 2002 a mountain biker on the Mendip Hills near Rowberrow came across the leg of a dog apparently torn from its body. This finding coincided with a number of reported sightings of a panther around Winscombe, just over the hills from Rowberrow.[6] On one occasion the farmers of Mendip organised

---

[4] *Western Daily Press*, 22 August 2001
[5] *Somerset County Gazette*, 18 December 2001
[6] *This is Somerset*, 2 May 2002

a hunt for what they had described as the Monster of the Mendips, in the wake of the discovery of a number of mutilated lamb carcasses.

So does the beast exist? Are the reported sightings the offspring of released exotic species now turned feral? Are those folk tales of 'big black dogs' related in some way to the modern experiences? Until someone produces a body or a well-defined photograph, the mystery continues.

Dead Woman's Ditch

❀

There is a beauty spot on the Quantock Hills which contains both murder and mystery. High above the village of Over Stowey, on the narrow roadway to Crowcombe, lies Dead Woman's Ditch, a popular meeting place for the Quantock Staghounds, and so named to reflect the terrible deed that took place there over 200 years ago. But since then history has almost repeated itself for in more recent years the body of another woman has been discovered here and subsequently the police searched this part of the Quantock Hills for yet another. The name of Jane Shorney may be long since forgotten other than by Somerset folk, but the names of Shirley Anne Banks and Suzy Lamplugh are much fresher, not just in local memory, but across the nation.

Jane Shorney

The tragic story of this beauty spot begins in 1798. John Walford worked as a charcoal burner on the Quantock Hills, a solitary existence but well suited to this quiet, handsome lad. He was popular in the nearby village of Nether Stowey, especially with Ann Rice, a real local beauty and the miller's daughter, to whom he was betrothed. His life revolved around a weekly routine of cutting and gathering coppiced timber for burning and then watching over the turf covered fire whilst the timber smouldered for a period of four to five days. During this time the charcoal burner would need to tend the fire every hour or two, leaving little time for sleep.

Against the background of this lonely life, Jane Shorney, the daughter of another charcoal burner, turned her attentions to young John. Under cover of darkness, she would visit his secluded hut on the hills, offering him comfort. Inevitably, with John succumbing to the girl's tempting ways, she found

Dead Woman's Ditch

herself expecting his child. It was incumbent upon John to forsake his fiancée, and on 18th June 1789 he and Jane were married.

Almost at once, married life became intolerable. Jane taunted John incessantly over the loss of his true love. Her constant intolerance and vindictiveness reduced him to a shrivelling wreck. If only he had stayed loyal to Ann. The situation came to a head on the night of 5th July when, after a heavy drinking session at the nearby Castle of Comfort Inn, she provoked him once too often.

On their way home, something snapped inside him. He took her by the throat and shook her uncontrollably. Then, wrenching a post from the hedge, he beat her unconscious with it, finally slitting her throat with a knife. Suddenly he realised just what he had done. Here was his wife of just over two weeks, limp in his arms. This was no premeditated act. Yes, keep her quiet, remove the source of the torment, but he had no intention of killing her.

Seeing no one was around, and wondering how to dispose of her body, he considered dragging her to a nearby well. The effort was too great, especially disadvantaged as he was with no light to work by. It was all he could do to drag her to a ditch beneath a small raised bank, the remains of an old Roman settlement. There he placed his wife in a shallow grave, covered with a few stones, branches and leaves. Inevitably the body would be discovered, buried so inadequately.

Within a few days, it was realised that no one had seen Jane, certainly not since the night of the big argument. Her father called for a search party to quarter the hills. And there in the remains of that prehistoric ditch, the body of Jane Shorney was later discovered.

John admitted his guilt immediately and was taken off to Bridgwater to await his trial, which, in the light of his confession, lasted just three hours. There was no alternative but to declare him guilty, and with that came the mandatory death sentence. He was to be hanged by the neck until dead and his body to be given to science. The judge wept as he announced his verdict – a reflection of the compassion he felt for this normally quiet man, driven to the extremes of human tolerance. But the public thought differently.

This had been a particularly violent period in Bridgwater's past. Numerous murders had occurred in the preceding years. Local people had suffered enough and required an example to be set. They demanded that John's body should be caged and hung from a gibbet for all to see for years to come. That surely would deter any would-be villains. The judge acceded to their request.

The following day, John was shackled around the neck, wrists and ankles and placed in a cart for the journey to Nether Stowey and beyond to his place of execution. When he arrived in the village, the preparations at the gibbet were not yet complete, and so John's torment was prolonged, as the party had to wait. The condemned man was passed a pint of the local cider.

The villagers, as was the custom on such occasions, had turned out in their family groups with their picnics. With the gibbet ready for the execution, the horse and cart carrying John Walford moved to the scene.

An excited buzz filled the air as the cart pulled up under the gallows. Then out from the crowd stepped John's first and only true love, Ann Rice. As one, the villagers realised the solemnity of the occasion and turned their backs. Ann walked forward, never taking her eyes off John. The villagers had realised this was Ann's moment to grant John forgiveness. A member of the execution party helped her up onto the cart and for a minute or two the young couple exchanged their final words, no doubt those of regret on the one part and forgiveness on the other.

As Ann leaned forward for a parting kiss, the executioner placed his arm as a barrier between them. Ann was quietly and respectfully lifted down from the cart. The horse's rump was slapped and the cart then pulled forward, leaving John's body dancing at the end of the rope.

His remains were placed in a cage and left hanging from the gibbet for a full year. The 30 ft tall gibbet, that high to ensure its visibility was certain over a wider area, was cruelly placed within clear view of the front door of the home of John Walford's mother. The crows, magpies and blowflies having taken what they could from the body, it was buried, still in its cage. Meanwhile, the gibbet remained until the next century when it was taken down and converted into gateposts.

Dead Woman's Ditch and Walford's Gibbet are now well known local landmarks, perhaps too well known and perhaps it was the very name of 'Dead Woman's Ditch' that attracted the attention of another lady killer.

Shirley Anne Banks

Almost 200 years had passed since the murder of Jane Shorney. In Bristol a young, attractive lady had been shopping. A till receipt found later showed that she had purchased a dress just before 7.30 pm on the evening of Thursday, 8th October 1987. Shirley Anne Banks was just twenty-nine years old when she and her orange coloured Mini car disappeared from a Bristol multi-storey car park during the early evening. She was not seen alive again other than by her killer.

The following afternoon an elderly couple were driving near the Clifton Suspension Bridge in Bristol, when they noticed smoke coming from Leigh Woods. Having slowed down to investigate, they heard what appeared to be the sound of a violent confrontation. Suddenly a man in dark clothing appeared, as if lit by a spotlight, where the sun broke through the canopy of trees. Shouting angrily at his victim, he rained blows with one hand as he stopped her escape with the other. The victim fell and a series of kicks were inflicted on the defenceless body.

The screaming stopped; the man leaned over his now silent companion and then looked around as if to see if any witnesses had taken in the event. Amelia Hart, the passenger in the car, opened the window and demanded to know what he was doing. The man's anger then seemed to turn on Mrs Hart as he raced towards the vehicle, hurling abuse and waving his fists in anger. The good lady wound up her window as rapidly as she could and her husband sped off before the same treatment was dished out to them.

Unbeknown at the time, they had just witnessed the murder of Shirley Banks. The killer, we are now aware, must have returned later to remove the body – but where to dispose of it?

It was three weeks later in Leamington Spa that 40 year old Carmel Cleary was the victim of an attempted rape by a man armed with a knife. Showing commendable presence of mind, she ran screaming from her boutique into the street, action that soon led to the arrest of her assailant, John Cannan. Officers searched his black BMW and his home. Items found in that search provided vital evidence to link him with an attempted robbery and rape. And in his garage was Shirley Banks' Mini, now fitted with false number plates.

John David Guise Cannan was born in 1954 and married in 1978. He proved to be an alcoholic and had a considerable number of affairs during his marriage. In December 1980 he had raped and almost murdered a girlfriend. In 1981 he raped a 37 year old pregnant lady in a Sutton Coldfield knitwear shop, having stripped his victim naked in front of her mother and young son. For this he was sentenced to eight years' imprisonment.

Suzy Lamplugh

In July 1986 John Cannan was released from the prison where his fellow inmates had nicknamed him Mr Kipper. Three days after his release, on 28th July, Suzy Lamplugh, a 25 year old attractive, blond and vivacious estate agent, vanished after meeting a client called Mr Kipper to view a property. Her car was found later that day, parked at an awkward angle, as if abandoned in a hurry, and with her purse still in the glove compartment. It was becoming clear she had been abducted and this was confirmed by the report of a neighbour close to the property to be viewed, who described hearing an argument outside the premises and seeing a man bundle a young woman into a car.

A nationwide search was triggered which caught the attention of the media, and Suzy Lamplugh became a nationally recognised name. Over two hundred police were involved in the enquiry. John Cannan had been interviewed and had been unable to provide an alibi for his whereabouts at the time of her abduction. In the months that followed, there was a series of West Country rapes for which John Cannan was interviewed.

Meanwhile, on 3rd April 1988, the body of Shirley Banks was found at Dead Woman's Ditch. The autopsy revealed that she had been bludgeoned to death and her skull crushed like a shell. But what brought her body to this location, a distance of some 40 miles from Leigh Woods, where she had met her tragic end? Clearly it was the choice of her killer – but why? Was he drawn by the name? Surely if he was familiar with the story behind the origin of the place name, he would know that the last murderer to use the spot had soon been caught and executed for his crime.

What could have been in his mind? And was this the only such occasion that he was to use the site?

On Wednesday, 5th April 1989, the twenty-three day trial of John Cannan for the murder of Shirley Banks commenced at Exeter Crown Court. Throughout this period not once did Cannan show any sign of emotion. The unanimous conclusion of the jury was that he was guilty of sixteen charges, his crimes including murder and rape, abduction and attempted kidnapping. He was sentenced to life imprisonment.

In December 2000 the media reported that police were interviewing John Cannan in connection with the abduction and murder of the missing estate agent Suzy Lamplugh, who had disappeared from her office on 28th July 1986 when she took her client Mr Kipper to view a property. This was not the first time he had been questioned in connection with this case. He was interviewed at the time of her disappearance and again in 1990.

Of what they discovered when they talked to him I have no idea, but I walk the Quantock Hills almost every day and, in April 2001, I witnessed a considerable police presence in the area of Dead Woman's Ditch. Some twenty police officers, including specialist search teams with dogs trained to find human remains, spent a week there carrying out an intensive search of the forested hillside, looking for the body of Suzy Lamplugh – by then nearly fifteen years after her disappearance.

A tragically afflicted beauty spot indeed.

A MYSTERIOUS
VICTORIAN SCANDAL

---------- ❂ ----------

During the latter part of the 19th century, various towns in Somerset witnessed occasional visits from the self proclaimed 'Son of God'. These appearances generated much interest and speculation. The Reverend Henry Prince, or 'The Blessed', as he was known to his followers, would arrive at the towns in a grand open-top carriage drawn by four large bay horses. He was protected on all sides by outriders wearing purple livery. Enormous bloodhounds ran before his carriage, close on the heels of a vanguard who loudly proclaimed: 'Blessed is he who cometh in the name of the Lord.'

The townsfolk, especially those of Bridgwater, generally considered the man and his followers to be harmless if not a little eccentric. He was, however, very wealthy and spent well in the locality. Clearly such people should be encouraged and protected from any unjust press criticism – and there was plenty of that to come.

The villagers of Spaxton generally felt the same way. It was there that the Reverend Prince and his community had set up their home, providing much needed work for the locals and prompt payment for the tradesmen. All their dealings with the outside world were of such a nature that they would not attract a bad reaction from village people. But the Church held different views on the practices apparently happening up on the Quantock Hills, and it was these that were to cause a massive, internationally-reported scandal.

Just what went on behind the high walls of their community was a mystery at the time. Although much was eventually revealed, a part, at least, remains a mystery even to this day.

Henry Prince, born in Bath, set out on a career in medicine. He qualified at Guy's Hospital but ill health intervened and he eventually followed a religious calling.

He took instruction at Lampeter College in West Wales, where he became such a zealot that his presence was an embarrassment. The problem for the college was that Prince had not actually done anything wrong; he had just become unbelievably pious and outspokenly critical. He had to go.

The vice-principal contacted the Bishop of Bath and Wales for help. Was it possible to find a small church at the back of beyond where Prince could be installed as a curate and do no serious damage to the ecclesiastical establishment? And so he was appointed to the curacy of a tiny church in the small village of Charlynch, a mile or so from Spaxton.

While the regular vicar was away in 1846 on indefinite holiday, Henry Prince had the opportunity to take the pulpit. He was a charismatic preacher and appealed to the lady members of the congregation. But it wasn't an easy beginning. The first few weeks saw virtually no one attending his services. No amount of threats of hell fire and damnation were going to wake up this sleepy congregation. Then he had a brainwave.

At one of his sermons, he stopped mid-sentence as though possessed. He threw himself about the church as if the spirit had taken him. The congregation were stunned and enthralled. He had declared himself to be the Son of God.

The following week the congregation's friends turned up in hopeful anticipation. Would the new vicar perform once again? And so the congregation grew, with all and sundry arriving, including many from the neighbouring towns. Some of those attending were of an unsavoury character and were there purely for the spectacle. For certain of the hardened drinkers of Bridgwater, it was good for a laugh: a few pints in town, out to the Lamb Inn at Spaxton for a couple more, and then off to the entertainment. The numbers attending increased so rapidly that separate services were held for the men and the women.

The size of congregations grew with each sermon and numbers had to be controlled. Prince divided his flock into the righteous and the sinners. The sinners were told to stay away. The righteous were predominantly female, good looking and wealthy. Those who were rejected as sinners were furious.

Families became split. Respected members of the community had lost their status. The Bishop of Bath and Wells was once again called in to deal with the problem of Mr Prince. This time the result was somewhat more serious. The Bishop revoked Prince's licence to preach within the diocese of Bath and Wells.

By this time Prince was already married. His first wife had been elderly and very wealthy. On her death, Prince inherited her fortune, and herein perhaps lay a clue as to the character and motivation of this man. Following the death of his wife, almost with no delay at all, he married Julia Starkey, the sister of a parish priest. The couple moved to the other side of the country, to Suffolk.

Whilst there, he continued his preaching and found more converts. The pattern followed that of Charlynch. The congregations were whipped into a frenzy, numbers grew by the week, the sinners were weeded out and inevitably the Bishop of Ely was called in to move the man on.

Amongst his congregation were the five very wealthy and middle-aged Nottidge sisters, each a spinster. Between them they had inherited a small fortune of £30,000. Three of them were sufficiently persuaded by Prince that they threw in their lot with him. The inheritance was a great help to Prince in his forthcoming campaign. He spent some while in Brighton and then Weymouth, preaching hell fire and damnation. Hundreds were persuaded to part with their money to serve the needs of the Lord. When sufficient funds had been acquired, two hundred acres of land were purchased in Spaxton.

And so it was that in the summer of 1846 a rather unusual community of people arrived in the village. They were well-to-do and rather grand in appearance. Soon the Agapemone (Greek for Abode of Love) was being developed. Behind 15 ft high walls, a twenty bedroomed house, gazebo, cottages and conservatory were erected. Another feature was the chapel. Unlike any other, it was luxuriously fitted out with velvet sofas and Turkish carpets. For an altar it had a billiard table.

Those who dwelt within were very private and well protected. But security was clearly not total. A fourth of the five Nottidge sisters joined the community once they were established at Spaxton, only to be kidnapped by her family under cover of darkness. The nearby villagers heard the screams but preferred to ignore the event. Back in the clutches of her family, she was committed to an asylum and thereby lost control of her share of the inheritance. It took Prince two years to track her down and, having found her, he convinced the courts that she was not mad and she was released into his care along with her inheritance.

In the wake of that breach of security, bloodhounds were introduced to deter any future invaders. Only local tradesmen had any real contact with those inside. They would deliver their goods to a hand which appeared through a hole in the wall. This may have been an unusual practice, but who cared when the business was significant in value and the accounts were settled so promptly?

Prince continued his recruitment campaign, bringing more women into his care. In all cases, the qualifications for joining the group were the same: single, good looking and wealthy. The looks were important to him because he saw it as part of his spiritual duties to 'purify' these maidens. Now it has to be said that 'purification' is something of a euphemism.   Within the community spiritual marriages were permitted, indeed dictated, by Prince. The married couples, however, lived separately, the

A pressman seeking admission to the Agapemone

men and women having different cottages. The younger, better looking women lived in the main house with Prince.

Henry Prince proclaimed that it was his responsibility to extend love from heaven to earth. A virgin had to be purified by the Holy Ghost, being of course himself. Nothing was left to the imagination. The act of purification was carried out by Prince and his spiritual bride performing naked in front of his followers, even his wife.

The act was known as the Great Manifestation. Before it happened, the virgins came to the altar draped in white. Prince examined each in turn and chose a Miss Paterson, who had grown up in the community since about five years old. She was then no more than sixteen and a beautiful young girl. Her clothes were removed and on the billiard table which served as the altar, she was deprived of her virginity.

Not all the followers found this practice acceptable. Many left the Agapemone, and the news slowly broke to the outside world of the happenings within the walls of the community. The press had a field day. The Church was scandalised; the people of Spaxton were inundated with press reporters but they all kept their lips sealed in respect of the little they did know about the Agapemonites. In time, the numbers leaving reduced and life was almost back to normal when another scandal was revealed.

The 'purified virgin' gave birth. This was not supposed to happen; indeed, it almost suggested that Prince was the same as any lesser mortal. Clearly she had been impregnated by the devil and a demonic immaculate conception had occurred. Outside of the walls, most people had a different opinion on the cause of the pregnancy, one that had a more natural basis.

In 1899 the 'immortal' Prince, at the age of 88, passed on. His followers were devastated. For an immortal to die was the ultimate sin. He was buried in the front garden at midnight in the upright position ready for the Resurrection day. His grave, along with those of the others buried there over the years, remains unmarked.

It was left to one of his disciples to identify a successor. The chosen one was the Reverend John Hugh Smyth-Piggott, a vicar from Clapton. And thus it was that unexpectedly at the end of one of his services in September 1902, he declared himself before his congregation to be the reincarnation of the 'Son of God'.

Many of those present were dumbstruck. Others immediately proclaimed him as their God and very convincing they were too.

Word spread far and wide. The press turned out in force for his next sermon, along with numerous objectors. Ugly scenes ensued outside the church and a police escort was required to get him safely home. The press soon picked up that Smyth-Piggott was to retire to a Somerset refuge, the Agapemone.

Established in his new role as the leader of the Agapemonites, Smyth-Piggott had an inventory produced of all his followers, showing their ages, interests and personal characteristics. Needless to say, it was announced that an intake of new and younger blood was required, female, of course. They had to be attractive both physically and financially. The money gained this way would be used to keep the community running, and their physical beauty would satisfy the more carnal needs of the Reverend Smyth-Piggott.

Although his wife was attractive enough, he felt the need to take a spiritual wife in addition. She was to be his chief soul bride, Ruth Anne Price. It was she who bore him three children: two boys and a girl called Glory, Power and Hallelujah.

The scandal resulted in him also being defrocked by the Church of England and the sect remained behind the walls of their Spaxton home. Visits from the Bishop of Bath and Wells in order to hand deliver the announcement were met with the news that the Messiah was away.

The press pushed hard to gather details. The Agapemonites stayed withdrawn in their shelter. The people of Spaxton remained tight-lipped. Years of charitable acts towards the villages, including generous gifts at Christmas, had bought their silence.

The scandal and gossip died down, and eventually Smyth-Piggott became a frequent and almost unnoticed visitor to the nearby towns. No longer the flamboyant horse-drawn carriage entry into the towns, now just a discreet visit by motor car when necessary. He certainly lacked the ostentatious style of his predecessor. On one of his visits, two Bridgwater men tried to tar and feather him, an act that landed them both with a spell in the local gaol.

Under Smyth-Piggott's leadership, the Agapemonites continued their comfortable, if unusual, lifestyle. As with Prince before him, he demanded total respect and obedience from all within his walls. Though lacking Prince's flair, he also attracted public interest and amusement. Bridgwater Carnival even had him featured as a tableau entry.

Smyth-Piggott's death came in March 1927, signalling the end of a community that had lasted over a hundred years. At its peak, over two hundred people were members. Even in its troubled days there had been at least sixty living there.

In 1958 the Agapemone was sold to a private developer and split into flats. No more secrecy surrounds the place and surely the days of international scandal are over for this small Quantock village. The chapel where the virgins were purified was turned into a glove puppet studio by two men who worked in partnership, producing educational films for the BBC. Spaxton quietly slipped back into its undisturbed way of life but left behind was a list of unanswered questions.

What else went on within those walls that never came to light? Just how many of the members were buried in upright coffins beneath the lawn? What will some future archaeologist make of that particular find?

FRENCH SPIES ON THE SOMERSET COAST

———————— ❀ ————————

The latter days of the 18th century were full of suspicion and intrigue. The French Revolution had seen the overthrow of the French aristocracy, and Napoleon's power was increasing. Across Britain the nation lived in fear of an imminent invasion by the French. In the West Country it was generally considered that the French navy could readily sail up the Bristol Channel and disembark their troops at a number of points along the Somerset coast. However, before any such invasion could be attempted, the French government would need good quality intelligence regarding the position of troops and any defensive positions in the area, along with details of the patterns of sailings in the channel.

Imagine you were responsible for the invasion. Consider the information you would require. Even if you had a competent spy keeping you up to date with land positions, you would also need information regarding shipping and its movements. After all, you could be on the brink of your attack when an English ship in the Bristol Channel spied your flotilla and raised the alarm.

The British government was well aware that such spying activity could be – and probably was – going on across the country, and it was important that the nation was alert to its duty to report any suspicious behaviour. And Somerset people felt that they had good reason to be alarmed. After all, hundreds were taken to the guillotine during the French Revolution, and rumours were rife, detailing graphically how women and children had been slaughtered. A lot of this was propagandist talk to ensure the nation remained united so that the French experience could not be repeated here. Much was made of the way the French behaved and how there was good reason to fear them. No one was safe in their beds whilst the French remained a menacing threat.

It was against such a background that the people of Nether Stowey reported the presence of a spy in their midst. This was a very conservative area with most of the land owned by two wealthy families. But two outsiders had recently entered the community. One, with a Devon accent, was reasonably well accepted and had been encouraged into the area by Thomas Poole, a respected Somerset businessman who owned and ran the local tannery business. He founded the Female Benefits Society and Men's Friendly Society. He was a good employer and almost above suspicion – but there was considerable doubt about the friends he kept.

The man from Devon, who came to the village on Tom Poole's invitation, was none other than Samuel Taylor Coleridge, the writer and poet. With Tom Poole's help, on the last day of 1796, he and his family settled in the village in a humble and somewhat squalid abode we know as Coleridge Cottage, a property now in the ownership of the National Trust. He was relatively popular in the village, not least with the ladies, since he charmed them with his poetic advances and once wrote of them that 'there are a number of pretty young women in Stowey, all musical … and I am an immense favourite'.

The other man, however, was not so well received. At Coleridge's suggestion he had been drawn to Somerset and was soon renting the far more expensive and palatial Alfoxden Park, just along the road in the village of Holford. This stranger was a different matter. Clearly he was a man of some independent means to afford such a property.

This second incomer had a foreign accent, probably French in the opinion of the members of this tight community. He didn't even dress like the locals, being more arty in his appearance and with a gypsy-like complexion. His sister, likewise, had a gypsy complexion and wild grey eyes and she wore old clothes suited to walking the hills rather than acting as the lady of the manor. This was just how the Nether Stowey folk expected the French to appear. And this stranger was inclined to avoid their company; he and the lady co-resident kept much to themselves. Surely that was evidence enough that he was up to no good. And who was the lady he lived with? They knew she was not his wife and doubted very much that she was his sister, as they had been led to believe. That was a likely story! In actual fact, the couple were William and Dorothy Wordsworth, close friends of Coleridge, and their accent was that of the north-west of England.

But it was the unusual behaviour of William Wordsworth away from Alfoxden Park that caused the greatest concern. This stranger would walk up onto the hills, to a high point with good all-round vision. There he would sit, mostly on his own, and take down notes as he looked out over the channel. From high on those Quantock Hills he could observe right across the water to South Wales. Every ship moving through the channel could be recorded and reported back to his French paymasters. Surely this was the behaviour of a spy. And then were would be times when he and Coleridge would disappear for days at a time, travelling on foot to Watchet, Porlock and beyond. Was this yet more intelligence-gathering activity? They were both great walkers, Coleridge in particular. He would walk the forty or so miles from Nether Stowey to Bristol and back to change his library books, the village not being that well blessed with literary material.

Alfoxton Park Hotel – home of Wordsworth

Back in Nether Stowey, Coleridge loved to receive visitors, and he and Thomas Poole entertained many intellectuals. Charles Lamb, William Hazlitt and Robert Southey, all great writers in their own right, were among those to visit Coleridge and Poole, and spend many an hour philosophising and sharing their thoughts. Another visitor was the scientist Davy, the inventor of the miner's lamp that bore his name. Yet another was John Thelwall, and, for many Nether Stowey residents, it was this visitor in particular who confirmed their suspicions. Thelwall, albeit acquitted, had been one of the defendants in the 1794 treason trials. No smoke without fire! What on earth could bring such a man to Nether Stowey unless some plot was afoot?

Meanwhile, in Alfoxden Park, a local man, Thomas Jones, who was acting as a waiter and gardener to the 'foreign' visitors, had reported his fears to the neighbourhood doctor regarding the integrity of his employers, referring to his suspicions about 'those French people'. The doctor passed the information on to the Home Office, and the government sent in James Walsh, a secret agent. He was to investigate these 'spies' and produce the evidence of their misdeeds.

And so, on 15th August 1797, Walsh took lodgings at the Globe Inn in Nether Stowey, right next door to the house of Thomas Poole. Now Coleridge's property and Thomas Poole's both had long gardens and although they were in adjacent streets, the gardens met at their bottom boundaries. This meant that Coleridge would spend much of his time in Poole's garden, in fact beneath a group of lime trees that were the inspiration of his poem *This Lime Tree Bower my Prison*. He also wrote in his notes: 'We have a very pretty garden and large enough to find us vegetables and employment. I am already an expert gardener ... We likewise have a sweet orchard and at the end of it T. Poole has made a gate, which leads into his garden.' This romanticised version of Coleridge's early days in the cottage does not fairly reflect the reality. He was a disaster as a gardener and spent little time at home, but, when he did, much of it was spent through that garden gate in the grounds of Thomas Poole's, where they spent many an hour conversing.

So it can be seen how convenient it was for the government agent to take up residence at the Globe, right next door to Poole's home. From his lodgings he could observe the gardens and

comings and goings of both men. It was also from there that he
gave out payments to any locals who were in a position to pass
on information of the whereabouts and activities of the strangers,
not least, of course, Wordsworth, from the next village. So it was
that Thomas Jones was now collecting pay from his employers at
Alfoxden House and also being paid for reporting their activities
to the government agent. Walsh, the agent, even followed them on
their walks on the Quantocks, hiding behind rocks and trees as he
did so.

He must have spent a considerable time walking those hills, for
both Coleridge and the Wordsworths would spend hours and
even days at a time there. Often they could be seen alone,
sometimes as a threesome with Dorothy, or many times Coleridge
and Dorothy Wordsworth as a couple. Certainly, Coleridge had a
great fondness for Dorothy despite having a wife and family back
at their humble cottage. Dorothy's company was far more
inspirational; they had so much in common and were clearly
much in tune with each other.

Regarding the matter of spying, the truth of the matter was
soon revealed. At the end of his investigations, the agent was able
to report that the strange couple at Alfoxden Park were William
and Dorothy Wordsworth, the poets who were later to come to
fame with Coleridge, their dearest and closest friend at the time.
The French accent was actually Cumbrian, which in the latter
days of the 18th century would have been like a foreign language
to some Somerset folk. The hours of copious notes taken on those
commanding viewpoints on the hills were simply the jottings of a
poet, penned in the peace and tranquillity of the Quantock Hills.
It was through the taking of such notes that the two great poets
between them began to develop the idea of the *Rime of the
Ancient Mariner*.

Coleridge lived for eighteen months in Nether Stowey and the
Wordsworths a year at Alfoxden Park. It was a period when the
threesome were almost one, sharing a love of poetry and each
feeding off the brilliance of the others. In that short period,
Coleridge and Wordsworth both created the greatest of all their
masterpieces. Never again were they to achieve such heights of
creativity. The *Rime of the Ancient Mariner*, *Frost at Midnight*,
Kubla Kahn and *Christabel* were just some of Coleridge's
achievements. Wordsworth penned *The Ruined Cottage*, *Lines*

Written in Early Spring, *The Last of the Flock*, *A Somerset Tragedy* and a whole host of others in this most prolific period.

Sadly, although the truth was now available, the local folk preferred to maintain their suspicions regarding the Wordsworths, and the couple were effectively ostracised. The renewal of their lease was declined by the owner under pressure from other locals. At the end of the agreed year's rental they joined Coleridge on a prolonged trip to Germany. Coleridge, already a heavy user of laudanum and other opiates, was never able to reproduce his former brilliance, and Wordsworth was unable to receive those previous sparks of inspiration.

Coleridge returned to Somerset, but only briefly in his later years, and one cannot help but think that there must have been a lingering bitterness at the way the local folk had treated his closest friends. The mystery had been resolved – but not as far as the folk of Nether Stowey were concerned. And perhaps they had good reason, for, unbeknown to them, Wordsworth's French connections were stronger than most had realised. Around the time of the storming of the Bastille, Wordsworth had spent a year in France as a supporter of the French Revolution. During that period he lived with a French woman as man and wife and on his return to England left behind him an illegitimate child.

So where did his loyalties lie? With the English or with the French? Could this explain his aloofness with the locals at Nether Stowey? Was he indeed, as well as a truly great poet, a spy after all?

THE NEIGHBOUR
FROM HELL

———————❁———————

Sheltered beneath the slopes of Exmoor, picturesque Porlock seems to have a climate and character all of its own. Its rugged cliffs and densely wooded headlands make it one of the most picturesque spots in the whole of the West Country. Colourful cottages line the streets, and amongst the inns, which are full of character, can be found the Old Ship, where the poet Southey is said to have written: 'Porlock, I shall forget thee not, Here by the unwelcome summer rain confined.' No wonder poets such as Southey and Coleridge were attracted to Porlock, together with nearby Porlock Weir, as indeed were William and Dorothy Wordsworth. It has a certain agelessness and charm which suggest peace and tranquillity.

But it was not always so. There was once a Saxon settlement, raided by the Danes, and it was in AD 918 that such a marauding horde was defeated by the stout locals. Violence returned again when in 1052 Harold Godwinson arrived with his fleet of nine ships and attacked and burned Porlock, killing thirty thanes, and then went inland pillaging, taking cattle and other property, and slaughtering many more of the local inhabitants. This was the Harold who, when King of England, was later to lose his life to a Norman archer at the Battle of Hastings. His justification for attacking Porlock seems to have been one of simple envy of Aelfgar, the son of Leofric, who was the popular leader of the region.

Such events demonstrate only too well how violence can lurk behind the gentle façade of sleepy towns and villages, violence such as that which was festering in the autumn of 1913 and came to a head the following summer, mirroring in many ways the violence which was erupting across Europe with the advent of the Great War.

For Porlock it all began on Hallowe'en night in 1913, when 55 year old Henry Quartly visited his neighbour, Mrs Fanny Pugsley. She lived with her husband in their home in Parson Street, a quiet road which leads to nowhere other than up into the steep-sided and heavily-wooded Hawk Combe and Doverhay Down. In this idyllic setting, something had caused Henry Quartly to lose his temper and, if we are to believe Mrs Pugsley, to use the foulest of language within her house. Such was the anger in his vitriolic outburst that Mrs Pugsley suggested it could be heard down on the main road.

These were the facts that she presented when her complaint was heard in the magistrate's court at Dunster on 3rd December 1913, a hearing which required both parties involved to make a 20-mile round trip for their troubles, only to be told that, as the result of insufficient evidence, the case was to be dismissed.

It's surprising how often a minor dispute between neighbours can become a lifelong feud, sometimes with such ferocity that they feature in TV programmes where the neighbours from hell for one group of people become the entertainment for another. Such would have been the case for Henry Quartly and the Pugsleys, for it seems that after the court case, the quarrel was to become the mother of all feuds. Henry Quartly completely changed in character, becoming sad and morose, manically depressive – and perhaps the warning signals were there for what was yet to come.

The feud simmered on into the summer, and once more Quartly had received a summons to appear before the magistrate in Dunster. Once more he would be obliged to complete the 20-mile round trip to hear the case against him. And surely once again the whole day would be wasted with yet another dismissal. It was all getting very out of hand, and his moroseness turned to anger and hatred, frustration and despair.

It was 3rd June 1914. The court case was approaching, with just two more days to go. It was a quiet enough day. Alice Middleton and Mrs Chapman were walking along the street and exchanged pleasantries with 59 year old Henry Pugsley as they passed by. Each, in their own chosen direction, continued about their daily business. It was a perfectly normal, quiet moment in the life of a village community. But then there came the loud crack of gunfire, and both Alice Middleton

Parson Street, Porlock

and Henry Pugsley lay in the road, Pugsley now seriously injured.

Henry Quartly, who had fired the shot, had all along been hiding in bushes in his garden on the other side of a 5 ft high wall. And it was there that he was to remain for the time being. George Bushen, another neighbour, meanwhile, had rushed out from his house at the sound of the shot, just in time to see Pugsley fall to the ground and his wife rush to his side.

The local police constable, Joseph Greedy, was summoned and it was not long before he arrived on the scene. Quickly assessing the situation, with Mrs Pugsley looking after her wounded husband and Alice Middleton still lying in the road, he realised the greatest immediate threat to everyone's safety remained with Henry Quartly. As Mrs Pugsley tended to her husband's needs, another shot was heard. This time from Quartly's house. Had he shot yet another person or was he now finishing off himself as well, such was the state of his disturbed mind on that fateful day?

It was soon apparent that the shot he had fired was intended for himself but had been unsuccessful. Outside his home, his sister screamed anxiously that, in the state of mind that he was in, Quartly would kill anyone who came near him. But PC Greedy was made of stout-hearted, West Somerset stock and bravely addressed the crisis head on. Into the house he ran and took a flying leap at the aggressor. As they both crashed to the ground and wrestled for the gun, PC Greedy managed to get to it first and then had the unenviable task of keeping Quartly pinned down until further assistance, which fortunately wasn't too long in coming, arrived in response to his calls for help.

PC Greedy had saved Quartly from his own self-destruction, and no doubt spared the lives of others on that day. Completing the arrest, Greedy took his prisoner to the police station in Dunster and there he was charged with shooting with intent to kill, for, at that stage, as far as Greedy knew, Pugsley was still alive. With the news of his death, the charge was upgraded to murder.

Quartly had objected to the need to travel the 20 miles to and from Dunster for his bad language case, but his trip to Taunton for his trial on 20th October 1914 was to have no return journey. No doubt well aware of the certain outcome of the trial and the sentence he could expect, he declined all offers for a solicitor to act on his behalf. When it was pointed out by the judge, Mr Justice Atkin, that there was no need for him to plead guilty, he responded that guilty he was and that was the beginning and end of it. And not only was he guilty of the murder of Henry Pugsley but his only real regret was that he hadn't killed Mrs Pugsley, too.

Such statements were clearly not going to endear him to the hearts of judge and jury. The verdict was a formality, as was the penalty: death by hanging.

On 10th November 1914 Henry Quartly was hanged at Shepton Mallet gaol by the infamous Thomas Pierrepoint, Britain's last professional executioner. Porlock, saddened and shocked by the loss of two of its community, learned to live with the terrible events of that fateful day. Others from the village were also to lose their lives in the years that followed but for them it was on the battlefields of Europe. Amidst the horrors of war, the Quartly affair soon became a thing of the past and Porlock slipped back into its otherwise tranquil ways.

AND DID THOSE FEET IN ANCIENT TIME?

———————— ✿ ————————

Perhaps Somerset's greatest unsolved mystery is wrapped up in the opening lines of William Blake's classic verse:

And did those feet in ancient time
Walk upon England's mountains green?
And was the holy Lamb of God
On England's pleasant pastures seen?

For it is in those words that one of the great mysteries of Glastonbury can be found. How many, I wonder, have sung the words of *Jerusalem* with no awareness that it is a reference to Christ and his legendary journeys to Somerset and Glastonbury in particular. But is it legend or historic fact? Therein lies the mystery. Was it at all possible that Jesus made the journey to Somerset? Where is the credibility in such a story?

The gospels tell us how Mary, the mother of Jesus, and her husband Joseph made the annual journey to Jerusalem at the time of the Jewish Feast of the Passover. Joseph was a carpenter and, hence, not a wealthy man. His family's trip would have been on foot, perhaps with the aid of a donkey to carry those items required for such a journey from their home town of Nazareth.

In Jerusalem, they would have met with old friends and family, many not having been seen since the same time the previous year. One such family friend was Joseph of Arimathea. He was a wealthy man, a merchant and a Roman citizen. Legend has it that he was the older brother of Mary's father, her Uncle Joseph.

It was on one such visit to Jerusalem, when the twelve year old Jesus was in the party, at an age when he was considered to be passing from boyhood into manhood, that his family were ready to start the journey home and had joined the large number of fellow Galileans. Jesus asked if it would be acceptable for him to visit the temple one more time and then catch up with his family later.

Mary and Joseph would have been travelling with groups of friends and relatives, providing some safety in numbers. As the Galileans made their way home, those with transport would have progressed much faster than those without, and the more aged walkers would bring up the rear of the migrating convoy, which would gradually have stretched itself out over a few miles.

After a day of travelling it was realised that the young Jesus had not caught up with his family, so Mary and Joseph, undoubtedly now very concerned, turned around to retrace their steps back to Jerusalem, hoping beyond hope that they would find Jesus somewhere further back in the convoy. But nowhere was he to be seen. The end of the convoy was reached and they continued to Jerusalem alone and away from their own people. They realised that in Jerusalem they would struggle to track down the young lad without assistance and thus they sought out Mary's Uncle Joseph to recruit some local help.

After three days without success, their search led them to the temple, where they found Jesus among the scribes and priests, who were amazed by his understanding and quest for knowledge. They all returned to Joseph's home in Arimathea before completing the journey home, and perhaps it was there that Joseph of Arimathea suggested taking Jesus under his wing. Here was a young lad with an enquiring mind and with a spirit of adventure. And here was his great uncle, a merchant who travelled the seas to foreign lands beyond the Mediterranean, beyond the limits of the Roman Empire as it was at that time. Why not take the lad with him on such a journey, broaden his experience and satisfy his thirst for knowledge?

Merchant traders travelling great distances did so by trading at ports along their journey. Jesus would visit many of the Mediterranean countries, pass through the Straits of Gibraltar, or the Pillars of Hercules as Joseph would have known them, out into the great ocean and onward to Britannia, where Joseph would trade for Mendip lead, silver and Cornish tin. What an opportunity for a 12 year old lad. What an educational experience.

If evidence is needed that such journeys took place, we have only to look to the town of Bridgwater where Phoenician ring money was found in the River Parrett, indicating their trading presence in the area. Legend has it that Jesus sailed with Joseph and proved a useful crew member by practising the carpentry skills taught him by his father. Through the Mediterranean they sailed, through the Straits of Gibraltar, into the great ocean, hugging the coastline of Spain, then north across the Bay of Biscay to arrive on these English shores at St Michael's Mount on the south coast of Cornwall. Here they traded for Cornish tin, exchanging goods acquired from the Mediterranean ports. Joseph and Jesus travelled into the heart of Cornwall to where Joseph knew he could increase his trade as on previous trips.

Their journey continued, around the treacherous western tip of Cornwall, past Hartland Point and Lundy, on to the western tip of the Mendip Hills, to Brean Down and the small port at the mouth of the River Axe. From here a group of Celts led them up onto the Mendips, to the lead mining village of Charterhouse. Onwards through Priddy they reached their journey's end at Glastonbury, undoubtedly the cultural centre of the West Country in those times, with a wide range of artisans practising their skills. After his return to the Middle East, Jesus returned to his parents, no doubt full of wonderful tales to tell.

By the time Jesus was in his early twenties, his father had died and Mary was living with a female relative. The Romans had entered a period within which Jews were being heavily persecuted with almost daily crucifixions. Britain lay beyond the rule of Rome. No wonder that Jesus decided, according to legend, to revisit our shores, but this time without his uncle and using his carpentry skills to earn his position in the crew. As on previous trips, the vessel would have called at the various ports en route, increasing the value of its cargo with each trade. And onwards to Britain, but this time to Glastonbury via the River Parrett. Jesus settled a while, built a house from wattle and daub and began to preach the message of his God. After two or three years, he returned home to Judea and there began his mission, with which we are more familiar through the stories of the New Testament.

Years later, Jesus was executed by crucifixion. It was Joseph of Arimathea who went to Pontius Pilate and requested his permission to have the body removed from the cross. This was granted, and, in seeking that permission, Joseph was once more

Glastonbury Tor, beneath which legend claims the Holy Grail is hidden

seen to be closely identified with Christ. This was a dangerous association, especially in the light of the rumours that soon followed regarding Christ's resurrection. The followers of Christ were to be rounded up and Joseph became a wanted man. His safety could only be found beyond the reach of the Roman Empire and so he returned to Britain and Glastonbury, just avoiding capture as the message spread from port to port across the Mediterranean of the need for his arrest.

On arriving back in Somerset, he walked the Polden Ridge to Wearyall Hill where, at the end of his journey, he planted his staff in the ground. There, given time, it took root and now it – or through a series of cuttings one of its offspring – still flowers every Christmas, a sprig being sent to the Queen. But herein lies no mystery, just nature playing its role with a plant from the Middle East taking root in a moister, wetter clime.

But where the mystery continues is in the legend of the chalice. This was the cup which Christ used at the Last Supper and which Joseph in escaping brought with him as a relic. Such was the importance of this relic, which held the wine that represented the blood of Christ, that it was necessary to hide it underground at the foot of Glastonbury Tor. This is the Holy Grail – which has yet to be rediscovered.

Fact or fiction? We shall never know. It will always remain Somerset's greatest and most lasting mystery.

THE UNPOPULAR CURATE

❀

The village of Old Cleeve lies to the south-west of the harbour town of Watchet. As a village, it was home to numerous generations of my ancestors going back at least as far as the 17th century, and it is at the start of that particular period that this tale belongs. The year was 1604 and the country was in the midst of religious and political unrest. Catholics and Protestants were vying for power and were sworn enemies to each other. It was a time when it was necessary to nail one's colours to one religious mast or another. Not only was there turmoil within the nation, but also ever present was the threat of invasion by foreign powers, Spain, in particular.

Old Cleeve and the neighbouring villages had once played a significant role in the religious life of the area. Whilst the village itself can boast a 15th-century church built on the site of a Saxon one, nearby is Chapel Cleeve, a former grange which once belonged to Cleeve Abbey. So here was a religious centre of some significance. And here, on Clyve Hill, stood a set of three beacons, one of a series positioned along the coast, to forewarn of any approaching invasion. One beacon would be lit if ships fewer than seven in number were spotted, two beacons if more, and three if an invasion was taking place that the locals were unable to repel[7]. The picture being painted is one of a quiet rural village, with deeply religious inhabitants and an underlying threat of violence to be resisted at all costs. As if in parallel, life at a more local level was about to reflect the national mood.

The incumbent rector of Old Cleeve was the Reverend Edward Brickenden. As rector, he was entitled to the 'perpetual patronage'

---

[7] From the Wolseley collection, Somerset Record Office, DD/WO 49/3

of Old Cleeve which meant he could live there forever and this was a right which he could pass on to his successor, whoever that might be. Within the family it was understood that this privilege, i.e. the post of rector and the perpetual patronage, would pass down to the rector's grandson, Peter Smethwicke, when the time was appropriate.

But events were to take a different course from that which the family expected, a course that brought anger to the churchgoers of Old Cleeve, no doubt my ancestors amongst them. The Reverend Brickenden had, as his curate, the Reverend Mr Trat, who was something of a religious zealot and a man who believed that the word of the Bible should be followed to the letter. This was somewhat in contrast to the general morals of the 17th century, which were relatively lax, even by modern day standards.

Hence, the Reverend Trat would stand in the pulpit on a Sunday and preach with conviction the word of the Bible as he emphasised each commandment and message from the good book, directing his stare in such a way that each recipient felt the message was a personal one. When Jesus said 'Let those amongst you who is without sin cast the first stone', he was fully aware that none of us is without sin to some extent, even if it is simply envy of what others have and we do not. Why do millions do the National Lottery, for example? The Reverend Trat had the ability to prick the conscience of his congregation – and they didn't like it.

Listening to a sermon and learning how to be a better person was one thing. Leaving the service feeling the victim of an accusation, founded or otherwise, was another. Members of the congregation began to believe that this man, through means fair or foul, was learning everything there was to know about their personal and professional business. Was there no privacy? One by one, the villagers were turning against this seemingly vindictive individual and would be quite glad to see the back of him. As his congregation diminished, so his enemies grew in number.

This period of hostility towards the new curate coincided with the discovery by Peter Smethwicke that his grandfather, the Reverend Brickenden, was to pass the rectorship and the perpetual patronage of Old Cleeve on to his new curate, the Reverend Trat, rather than, as expected, to him. This was a major blow to Smethwicke who had looked forward not least to the

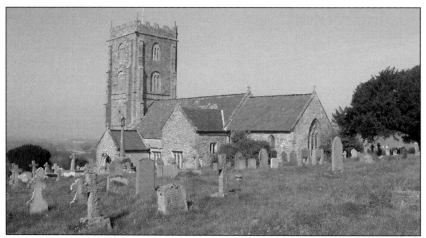

Old Cleeve church

guarantee of a home forever in the village. The resentment he felt towards his grandfather turned to anger, hatred and despair. How could this reversal of fortunes be turned back in his favour?

Character assassination seemed to be the simplest and most effective campaign strategy. Amongst Trat's former congregation, various members made accusations against him and rumour led to rumour. But some of his adversaries took more positive actions to discredit him. Peter Smethwicke's father, and almost certainly others, took to impersonating the curate. The Reverend Trat wore a very distinctive hat and cloak, and in this fashion travelled around the parish and neighbouring villages. He was easily recognisable simply from his profile as he rode across the hills.

At least one of his impersonators, dressed in the required fashion, followed women into the woods which still abound locally and there harassed those good ladies, who then reported their experiences to the local magistrate. Unfortunately for his adversaries, the only evidence against the reverend gentleman was the similarity of his dress to that of the aggressor. When Trat's wife tragically died in a drowning incident, the locals must have thought that their luck had changed at last. Poor Mrs Trat, whilst in Blue Anchor Bay, had become cut off by the incoming tide and sadly drowned. All kinds of allegations were made suggesting that this situation had been manipulated by her husband – but all to no avail.

Subterfuge having failed, desperate measures were called for. Peter Smethwicke gathered three of his closest and most trusted friends around him: Cyril Austen, Andrew Baker and Alice Walker. Between them they plotted the reverend's final downfall.

The parish of Old Cleeve was sparsely populated and spread over a wide area. Frequently this would necessitate the reverend trekking by horse over considerable distances. On one such trip the gang of three waited, concealed in a ditch. As Reverend Trat approached, they sprang from their hiding place, dragged him from his horse and stabbed him to death.

Now came the problem of disposing of the body. One would think there were ample places up on the moors around Old Cleeve to hide it but for some reason the perpetrators of this crime took the victim to his home where, since the death of his wife, he had lived alone. And it was here that the gruesome method chosen to dispose of his body began. His head and four limbs were all removed. The head was then cremated as best as they were able but at least it was now unrecognisable. The torso was put into a container large enough to take it and, after adding salt and water, Alice boiled the contents.

For the time being all the remaining bits were left in the reverend gentleman's house. After a week or two with the Reverend Trat failing to fulfil his duties, the alarm was raised and the police broke into his home to discover the gruesome remains of someone's unrecognisable body. And perhaps now we can start to understand what was going through the minds of his killers when they returned the body to the house.

If it was unrecognisable, it could be anybody's remains – perhaps those of a tramp. The Reverend Trat was already the victim of vitriolic rumours to the extent that anyone could now believe he was not just a woman molester but a murderer as well. Surely this was the body of one of his victims and the Reverend Trat had now fled the district to avoid capture and inevitable execution. But for this story to be believed, the local police would need to be convinced that the curate was still alive. And so to complete the illusion, Peter Smethwicke's father donned the hat and cloak one more time and rode through and beyond the village as if the curate were effecting his escape.

And perhaps the ruse would have worked, except for one fatal flaw in the gang's planning. When the police broke into the Reverend Trat's home, they discovered the hat and cloak still hanging in their usual position. Suspicion now fell on the tellers of the story, and each was detained for questioning. During various searches the skull was discovered, along with a pot full of blood.

Now, in those days, it was common practice in the case of a violent murder for the menfolk of the village to file past the body of the victim. Typically the body would be placed in a coffin and then propped up against a wall in such a way that the body was almost upright. It was somewhat reminiscent of those old sepia photos of the Wild West where notorious villains were left in open coffins outside the undertaker's window, placed there on public display. The principle behind this custom in the West Country was the firm belief that if the menfolk of the village each walked past and in so doing touched the corpse, then, when the killer made contact, the corpse would bleed.

Of course what happened in practice was that, so strong was the belief in this superstition, the guilty party would break into a cold sweat and run away, thus revealing his guilt. And perhaps that explains what happened next in the investigation of the murder of the Reverend Trat. As the police officer passed the pot of blood to Andrew Baker he dropped it, convincing the policeman of his guilt. He was arrested along with Peter Smethwicke. Cyril Austen revealed his involvement by fleeing the village, only to be captured later with an incriminating piece of bloodstained clothing.

In time, all four villains were arrested and delivered up for trial. Despite their pleas of innocence, the four were found guilty and hanged on 25th June 1604, from the gallows at the appropriately named Stonegallows, just outside Taunton. Meanwhile, Peter Smethwicke's father was imprisoned for his part in the impersonation of the curate.

THE MAN WHO INSPIRED THE STORY OF FRANKENSTEIN

———————————— ❋ ————————————

The sleepy village of Broomfield, set amidst the narrow winding lanes of the Quantock Hills, is perhaps best known today for the manor house of Fyne Court. Arranged around the green, where the annual All Saints' Day fairs were held for more than six hundred years, are rows of quaint cottages, the ancient village church and the grounds of Fyne Court. It is a rural setting which evokes images of days gone by: horse-drawn farm trailers moving slowly along the lanes, and shepherds quietly leading their flocks on their way to the distant market towns.

In stark contrast to that idyll, many years ago an experiment took place inside the manor which seemed to defy the laws of nature and the results of which even today remain wrapped in mystery. For within its walls, Andrew Crosse appeared to have created living organisms simply from the electrification of a mixture of chemical compounds. There were many who gave great credence to the outcome of this particular experiment, and such was its impact that Mary Shelley was inspired to write the story of Frankenstein.

Andrew Crosse was born on 17th June 1784. His family had considerable wealth and at one time owned five hundred acres of Broomfield, with many tenant farmers in their employ. Their home was 17th-century Fyne Court, a large property which lay sheltered in a hollow, just north of the village green. Most of the old manor house was destroyed in a disastrous fire in 1898, and what remains is now in the ownership of the National Trust and is leased to the Somerset Wildlife Trust. Ironically, the only part of the house that still exists is the part in which Andrew Crosse conducted his electrical experiments.

Fyne Court

Andrew Crosse was a pioneer of electrical research and was known locally as the Wizard Crosse; consequently his home was best avoided especially in the hours of darkness. To assist his electrical experiments, he constructed a network of 600 metres of copper wire through the tree tops around the grounds of his home. These all interconnected and linked in turn to a metal conductive pole which was positioned in such a way that it projected up vertically through the branches of one particularly large tree. The metal rod can indeed still be seen today – most easily in winter when the leaves have fallen. From this, a cable led into the music room.

Crosse discovered that during violent storms he could capture the electrical energy and this would light up the various pieces of apparatus in his laboratory. This earned him yet another title – 'The Thunder and Lightning Man'. There were many locals who described how they had seen the Devil dance along the wires and into the house. This was not a safe place to visit for the faint hearted, and the local farmers had their share of complaints as well. Needless to say, whenever there was a thunderstorm which affected their harvesting, Andrew Crosse was to blame. He had a passion for his experiments and for thunderstorms and often expressed his frustration when storms appeared to follow the meandering line of the River Parrett rather than heading towards his Broomfield home.

Subsequently, his house became more like a laboratory than domestic premises. Whilst this perhaps sounds like the life of a single man, his work was enthusiastically supported by his second wife, Cornelia (his first wife having died). Cornelia was a more than willing assistant and the knowledge she gained at his side was sufficient to enable her to write up his experiments after his death. However, her attitude to his melting down the family silver to produce the materials for his experiments has never been recorded. Even the glass and Wedgwood chinaware were not beyond his reach. Most of his experiments were carried out in the music room, which now serves the community as the Andrew Crosse Hall, much used by the Wildlife Trust for lectures and displays.

In this room various experiments were tried, including one where the wire leading from the copper wire network in the tree tops was connected to an enormous brass ball suspended over two Leyden jars, which, according to the weather conditions, would become electrically charged. One experiment, in particular, was to capture the world's attention. He appeared to have created a form of insect from a chemical solution. It seemed he had created life itself.

A piece of volcanic stone had been soaked in hydrochloric acid. A solution of flint and potassium carbonate was then placed onto it. An electrical charge was passed through this in an attempt to create silicate crystals. In Andrew Crosse's own words:

I constructed a wooden frame, of about 2 feet in height, consisting of 4 legs proceeding from a shelf at the bottom, supporting another at the top, and containing a third in the middle. Each of these shelves was about 7-inches square. The upper one was pierced with an aperture, in which was fixed a funnel of Wedgwood ware, within which rested a quart basin on a circular piece of mahogany placed within the funnel. When this basin was filled with a fluid, a strip of flannel, wetted with the same, was suspended over the edge of the basin and inside the funnel, which, acting as a siphon, conveyed the fluid out of the basin, through the funnel, in successive drops.

The middle shelf of the frame was likewise pierced with an aperture, in which was fixed a smaller funnel of glass, which supported a piece of somewhat porous red oxide of iron from Vesuvius, immediately under the dropping of the upper funnel. The stone was kept constantly electrified by means of 2 platina wires on either side of it, connected with the poles of a Voltaic battery of 19 pairs of 5-inch zinc and copper single plates, in two porcelain troughs, the cells of which were filled at first with water and 0.3% of hydrochloric acid, but afterwards with water alone.

I may state here, that in all my subsequent experiments relative to these insects, I filled the cells of the batteries employed with nothing but common water. The lower shelf merely supported a wide-mouthed bottle, to receive the drops as they fell from the second funnel. When the basin was nearly emptied, the fluid was poured back again from the bottle below into the basin above, without disturbing the position of the stone. It was by mere chance that I selected this volcanic substance, choosing it from its partial porosity; nor do I believe that it had the slightest effect in the production of the insects to be described.

Two weeks of experimentation had proved unsuccessful. The awaited crystals had failed to materialise but in their place was a number of very small mites.

Had he created life from chemical matter? Was he playing God? These were not the questions he himself was asking but they were the questions raised by his critics once news of the experiments broke out. He was simply reporting the results of the experiment as he saw them. Without justification, the news rapidly spread that it was Andrew Crosse himself who was claiming to have created life. In fairness, he had made no such claims and was conscious of the criticism to which he would be subjected if he misreported the outcome of these tests. The religious world was up in arms with the alleged claims of this mere mortal. It was, to them, a denial of the existence of God.

So Crosse was in no rush to go public with his findings. Such was the furore in scientific circles, however, in the wake of the rumours about his work, that in December 1837 he was requested by the Electrical Society of London to submit the details of his experiment and to make clear his position and his understanding as to what had taken place. He was clearly disturbed by this command and by the way he had been misrepresented, as shown in the following address to the association.

I must state, not for the sake of myself (for I utterly scorn all such misrepresentations), but for the sake of truth and the science which I follow, that I am neither an 'atheist', nor a 'Materialist', nor a 'self imagined creator', but a humble and lowly reverencer of that Great Being, whose laws my accusers seem wholly to have lost sight of. More than this, it is my conviction that science is only valuable as a means to a greater end. I can assure you, sir, that I attach no particular value to any experiment that I have made, and that my feelings and habits are much more of a retiring than an obtruding character; and I care not if what I have done be entirely overthrown, if truth be elicited.

A report of the experiment later appeared in the *American Journal of Science and Arts* (January 1839):

On the fourteenth day from the commencement of this experiment I observed through a lens a few small whitish excrescences or nipples projecting from about the middle of the electrified stone. On the eighteenth day these projections enlarged, and stuck out seven or eight filaments, each of them longer than the hemisphere on which they grew.

On the twenty-sixth day these appearances assumed the form of a perfect insect, standing erect on a few bristles which formed in its tail. Till this period I had no notion that these appearances were other than an incipient mineral formation. On the twenty-eighth day these little creatures moved their legs. I must now say that I was not a little astonished. After a few days they detached themselves from the stone and moved about at pleasure.

In the course of a few weeks about a hundred of them made their appearance on the stone. I examined them with a microscope, and observed that the smaller ones appeared to have only six legs, the larger ones eight. These insects are pronounced to be of the genus Acarus, but there appears to be a difference of opinion as to whether they are a known species; some assert that they are not.

I have never ventured an opinion on the cause of their birth, and for a very good reason – I was unable to find one. The simplest solution of the problem which occurred to me was that they arose from ova deposited by insects floating in the atmosphere and hatched by electric action. Still I could not imagine that an ovum could shoot out filaments, or that these filaments could become bristles, and moreover I could not detect, on the closest examination, the remains of a shell ...

I next imagined, as others have done, that they might originate from the water, and consequently made a close examination of numbers of vessels filled with the same fluid: in none of these could I perceive a trace of an insect nor could I see any in any part of the room.

If these creatures were acari, then strictly speaking they were arachnids (mites and spiders) and not true insects. But that is of little relevance. What matters is the apparent creation of life. Mary Shelley, the writer, attended one of Crosse's lectures given in London. Whilst it seemingly inspired Mary Shelley to create her story about Frankenstein, others took a different attitude and were positively aggressive in their 'vitriolic tirades', as Crosse described them. Under such public scrutiny and such a large and venomous backlash to his experiment, he chose to withdraw from public life 'shunned by and shunning – the world', which is a great shame and a sad loss, since here was a man seeking to learn and to push forward the boundaries of science.

This man of vision in 1836, while addressing the British Association for the Advancement of Science at a meeting in Bristol, declared that through the use of electricity 'we shall be enabled to communicate our thoughts instantaneously with the uttermost parts of the earth'. Perhaps this was just taken as a throw away line by the audience, but it demonstrates well the foresight of Andrew Crosse.

Other eminent scientists, at the request of learned bodies, were to successfully repeat his experiments, including a fellow researcher, W. H. Weeks, and in 1909, the eminent physicist Sir Michael Faraday. Whilst members of the scientific fraternity cried out for more explanation, well over a century later the phenomenon remains an unexplained mystery.

Andrew Crosse died at Fyne Court, in the same bed in which he was born, on 6th July 1855, aged 71. The epitaph chosen by his wife read: 'He was humble towards God and kind to his fellow creatures.' Whilst the mystery of his creation persists, his name has sadly faded from popular memory. The life of Andrew Crosse, though, is perhaps reflected in the classic horror story of Frankenstein, in which a man creates life and then watches it destroy him.

CHILD KILLERS

———————— ✿ ————————

Murder has never been nor should it ever be acceptable to society. But there is something doubly abhorrent when the victim of such a heinous crime is a child as the following stories will demonstrate all too clearly.

The Kent family tragedy

Who can imagine what goes through the mind of someone who has the capacity to slit the throat of an innocent three year old child and then place its body in an outdoor privy? What kind of insanity prevails for such an act? But this was exactly what happened in the village of Rode in North Somerset in the early hours of the morning of 30th June 1860. The life of Samuel Kent, the father of the family, was full of tragedy and here was another, with the murder of his son. This could have been his final tragedy but more was yet to come.

Samuel Kent was born around 1794, in Middlesex, and later he was to marry Mary Ann Windus, several years his junior. The couple settled in Finsbury, where a daughter, Mary Ann, taking her mother's name, was born in 1831, and a year later, another daughter, Elizabeth. There then followed a series of births with most of the children dying in infancy. By 1844 the family had moved to the Devon seaside resort of Sidmouth, perhaps in the hope of a healthier environment in which the offspring would stand a better chance of survival, but certainly on medical advice after an illness suffered by Samuel Kent himself. Daughter Constance was born in 1844 and William Saville Kent, their first surviving son, in 1845.

Around this time, Samuel Kent became a factory inspector, a most unpopular job, especially where factory owners were concerned. But it was a deeply necessary role in those Dickensian days of dark, gloomy and inhospitable mills and factories. It was an undertaking that was to take him further afield and back into the industrialised areas of Bristol and Bath. By 1851 the family had settled in Clevedon Road, in Walton-in-Gordano, and there Samuel lived with his wife and four surviving children, Mary Ann, Elizabeth, Constance and William Saville Kent.

During the years of their marriage, Mrs Kent had shown increasing signs of mental illness, as a result of which she was unable to cope with the upbringing of their young children, and so a governess was employed, Miss M. Pratt. By all accounts quite buxom, young and attractive in appearance, she lived in with the family, as did two teenaged servant girls.

This gives some idea of the relative comfort in which the Kents lived, albeit with the burden of four young children and a wife in increasing need of attention. It was here that the family's apparent improving fortunes were to take a turn for the worse yet again. First Mrs Kent's problems worsened and she died in 1852. Following her death, and there is no suggestion of impropriety in what I am about to say, Mr Kent married Miss Pratt, who by this time had been with the family for ten years and was now in her early thirties.

From Clevedon Road, the new family, once again with a mother, moved to Rode Hill House, now known as Langham House, in the grey-stone village of Rode, some four miles from Frome and eight from Bath. In the years that followed, the marriage was blessed with three more children, including a son, Francis Saville Kent, very much a favourite with his father. With a fourth child on the way, Samuel employed Elizabeth Gough as a nurse for the younger members of the family. Resentment towards the new mother grew from the older children of the first marriage.

Constance's behaviour took such an aggressive turn that she was packed off to school, along with her younger brother William. It was as if the old family was being ostracised. Such was their hatred for the new regime that, on one occasion, William and Constance ran away to Bristol, Constance cutting her hair to resemble a boy; her locks were later discovered in the outdoor privy.

As if there wasn't enough conflict within the family, on the outside there were those aplenty with vindictive wagging tongues who painted the worst possible picture of any event. In his role as a factory inspector, Samuel Kent was required to identify where unsafe practices were being applied. To put things right invariably added to the cost of running factories such as those of the cloth manufacturers in his part of north Somerset. In serious cases he could order the cessation of business until dangerous aspects were rectified. In such situations, the workforce would lose their ability to earn a living. And so a factory inspector's lot was not a happy one and enemies could be found amongst both the bosses and the workforce.

Back in their homes, those who found this gent's activities unpopular would no doubt have plenty to say about the death of his first wife and his marriage to the next. Did he murder his first wife to gain the heart of the second? Such were the unpleasant suggestions and innuendos being spread around the local community. Further unpopularity was caused when, in order to gain some privacy for his household, Samuel erected high fencing. What was this man trying to hide? As though rubbing salt in the wound, he then banned the locals from fishing along a length of stream for which he now paid rent. Giving him the benefit of the doubt, he was probably just seeking a quiet life. But it all added fuel to the fire on which simmered local hostility, as though everyone was just waiting for the day his three year old son was to be murdered.

On Friday 29th June 1860, the family retired to bed as usual. Up on the top floor were the housemaid and cook. On the second floor were four occupied bedrooms. In the master bedroom were Mr and Mrs Kent, with a new born daughter in a crib and across the landing was the room where Elizabeth Gough slept with the young lad Francis and the Kents' one year old daughter. Sixteen year old Constance and fifteen year old William, back home for the school holidays, also had their own rooms on the same floor.

It was in the early hours of the morning on Saturday, 30th June, that young Francis, the son from the second marriage, was lifted from his cot and wrapped in a blanket, then taken downstairs and apparently out through a window, across the road to an outdoor toilet where his throat was slit. His body was thrown into the well of the privy, where it lodged on a splashboard beneath the toilet seat. Who could possibly have carried out such a dastardly deed?

Elizabeth Gough awoke at five in the morning to discover the empty cot and her initial reaction was to assume that Mrs Kent had collected the child, as she occasionally did, and Elizabeth returned to her bed for an extra hour's sleep. She then dressed and went to her mistress's bedroom to collect Francis and prepare him for the day. It was then that the household was alerted. Realising that the drawing room window was open, a burglary or kidnapping was suspected and Samuel rushed off to fetch the police from Trowbridge, across the border in Wiltshire, whilst other members of the household called on their immediate neighbours to help in the search for the child.

The locals, despite their dislike of the family, willingly joined the search and it was two villagers, William Nutt and Thomas Benger, who found the poor little fellow's blood-drained body in a privy across the road from the family home. Initially it was just a pool of blood they saw, which suggested they were looking in the right place. Peering down into the darkness of the cesspit, they could see nothing. Nutt went for a lamp and as Benger's eyes grew accustomed to the dark, he spotted and retrieved a bloodstained blanket. When Nutt returned with the lamp, they were able to see the body lying on a splashboard which Samuel Kent had recently installed. The board had prevented the child's body from descending into the sewage.

The throat had been slashed to such a depth that the head was all but severed. Stab wounds were found on the body which the coroner later discovered to have been caused by a blade passing between two ribs and then being twisted and turned internally, although the child was already dead by that time. Shortly after the body was taken back to the house, Samuel Kent returned, with Inspector Foley and other police officers, to be told of the devastating news.

And thence began the quest to discover the murderer of this innocent child. But what were the clues to guide the investigators? Inside the house was the empty cot with a blanket missing. If an intruder had taken the child with the intention of its murder, would it bother wrapping it in a blanket? The drawing room window was opened. If the murderer was one of the household, why would they open a window instead of using the door? The door was unbolted from the inside, suggesting perhaps an inside job.

Outside, in the yard, the family dog had been doped. Would a member of the family need to dope the dog? In the privy was found a blood-spattered copy of the *Morning Star*, apparently used to wipe the knife used in the killing. This was not a paper taken by anyone in the household. There was such a confusion of evidence, some pointing to a culprit from within the family circle, other evidence suggesting an intruder.

For the locals, there was never any doubt. Samuel Kent was the villain of the piece. As sure as he had murdered his first wife, he had murdered his own son. No doubt, even today, attitudes would be much the same. We all recognise that most murdered children are the victims of family or friends. Why should this case be any different?

The world at large took a different view, and the press in particular favoured someone from outside the area and this was perhaps borne out by four similar recent murders, in each case the victim's throat having been cut. Many wondered if this was the 'Slasher's' fifth victim.

Unfortunately, it appears that the incompetence of Inspector Foley led to the prolongation of this whole affair by the destruction of vital pieces of evidence in the period immediately after the discovery of the crime. When one of his officers found a bloodstained nightdress stuffed into a boiler, in an apparent attempt to burn it, and when a bloodstained handprint was found on the window, he ordered his policemen not to be so insensitive to the distress of the family and allowed the nightdress to be returned to the boiler, and he himself wiped the window clean!

At the later inquest, members of the family and their neighbours were questioned. These included the nursemaid, Elizabeth Gough, who must have felt grief at the loss almost as great as any member of the family. Spectators in unison audibly drew breath as the state of the child's body was described. It was clearly a traumatic time for all concerned. The additional upheaval caused by the enquiry was recognised by the Revd Mr Peacock, who not only was a friend of the family but also was the foreman of the jury and it was in that latter capacity that he appealed successfully to the coroner for the family's feelings and emotions to be respected and for the cross-examination to be brought to a speedy end. With the case curtailed in this fashion, there was little option but to return a verdict of wilful murder by a person or persons unknown. It was an unpopular verdict, which was to stir up local feelings far more than anticipated.

The neighbouring population, convinced of the guilt of Samuel Kent, considered that the Revd Peacock, as a close family friend, had manipulated the jury and coroner alike. They could almost forgive the jury, for they were people just like themselves, but how could the coroner allow the villain to escape prosecution in this way? There was great pressure on Inspector Foley to effect an arrest. But he couldn't believe a member of the family could have committed the deed and so arrested Elizabeth Gough. What a terrifying and traumatic experience to have a child taken when in your care for it to be brutally murdered, and then to be accused of the deed. And there was no evidence to suggest any motive for Elizabeth to kill the child. It was not long before she was released and once again the public screamed for an arrest.

And so, on 15th July, Inspector Whicher of Scotland Yard was called in to take over the investigation. Every possible barrier to his progress was put in his path by Foley and the local force, but this man was from more determined stock than the local boys. He persisted and interviewed all the servants past and present and through this realised that the older children from the first marriage resented what they saw as an excess of love and attention being given to the children of the new wife. This was especially so in the case of Constance. Whicher was convinced of her guilt but lacked the evidence for a conviction.

During his interviews, a laundry maid told how Constance had gone to the laundry on the day the child disappeared and asked her to fetch her nightgown because she had left a purse in its pocket. As she was about to retrieve the gown, the laundry maid was sent to get a glass of water instead, and, during the time that she was away, both Constance and the gown had disappeared. But why would Constance want to remove a gown from the laundry when we already know that a nightdress was being burned in the boiler? The nightdress Constance took from the laundry was a ruse. If a nightgown had disappeared from the laundry, then Constance could account for there being one short in her wardrobe. Whicher had spotted the clue and arrested Constance on 20th July. Throughout questioning, Constance gave away no indication as to her possible guilt, and, on 27th July, the evidence at her court case was insufficient to prove the case and she was released. Once again, Elizabeth Gough was put back in the frame, arrested, tried and released.

During this period the press had descended on the otherwise quiet village of Rode in much the same way as they do today for a major media event. Such was the pressure that the family moved away, first to Weston-super-Mare while their house was sold, and then to Llangollen in Wales.

Constance was sent to a convent in France in the early part of 1861. In August 1863 she returned to England and went as a paying guest to a religious retreat in Brighton. The following year, she took the decision to confess her guilt. Accompanied by the Revd Wagner, the director of the retreat, she went to Bow Street magistrates' offices and confessed to the murder.

She appeared for trial at Salisbury Assizes on 21st July 1865, pleading guilty. As the written confession was read, Constance broke down in tears of remorse. Such was the emotion of the occasion that jury and judge alike also broke down in tears. Constance lifted the dark veil from her face as the judge passed sentence. Putting on his black cap he pronounced the penalty of death. Because she was just sixteen at the time of the crime, this was commuted to life imprisonment. In 1885, after an initial spell in Portland Prison, she was released from Millbank Prison aged 41 and, although theories exist, her whereabouts beyond that are uncertain. Some think she emigrated to a new life in New South Wales, under the name of Ruth Emilie Kaye. Others believe she

Constance Kent

inherited her mother's insanity and moved to London, where, in the years that followed, women in the East End died from horrific mutilations. Was 'Jack the Ripper' really 'Jill the Ripper'? Might the police have found the Ripper had they been looking for a woman rather than a man, or is that one speculation too far? Or did she simply retreat yet once more into the sanctuary and solitude of a convent? It remains a mystery.

The Tragic Case of Doris Brewer

It was 1933, between the wars. West Hatch was a quiet village unaccustomed to scandal and public attention. There was a small village shop that sold groceries and other daily requirements. Bread was still delivered by horse-drawn wagon from nearby Curland, and each Thursday a lad on a bike would wend his way from door to door taking weekly orders for groceries to be delivered by van on the Monday from the larger store of Paul and Hooper in Taunton.

The village school was attended by some sixty or so pupils, cared for by three teachers. Summer was always an exciting time for their pupils with days off at harvest time and the annual charabanc outing to Weymouth or Weston-super-Mare. It was a happy school, divided into three sections. First there were the mixed infants, with sand trays and beads for the new intake to play with until they progressed to chalks and slates. When they were ready for pencil and paper and eventually nib pens with real ink, they progressed to the segregated boys' and girls' juniors. In the playground a high wall separated the boisterous boys from the girls, who played hopscotch and with whips and spinning tops.

Here they learned sums and scriptures, history and geography, needlework and craftwork, with cane and leather craft also on the curriculum. On reaching the age of eleven, the scholarship examinations were taken in March, and those who passed progressed to the secondary school, whilst the others remained at the local school until they were 14 years old and then went out to work.

This was the village school scene for young Doris Winifred Brewer who was much the same as any other local lass – with one exception.

Doris lived with her grandmother in Slough Green and was pregnant at the tender age of 12 years old. It appears that the father was her uncle, 34 year old Frederick Morse, who lived in the same house. If this situation in itself was not tragic enough, the events that followed certainly were. It was 23rd February 1933, about ten o'clock in the morning. Young Doris was walking arm in arm with her uncle towards nearby Curry Mallet, and what was going through their minds we will never know, but we have to consider the possibility of a suicide pact. The shame attached to being an unmarried mother is perhaps less easy to understand today but was sufficient in those days for families to often disown daughters in such a condition. And to be thus at the age of twelve brought even greater shame on the family. But what if the father were a family member, the live-in uncle? This brought still more shame on the girl and disgrace to the household. Was this enough to drive the couple to plan suicide?

At about 10.20 am, they reached the Bell Inn in Curry Mallet, where Frederick Morse drank a quart of beer and purchased a half bottle of rum and a bag of crisps. Little is known as to what happened during the several hours that followed and here we have to speculate based on the proposals put forward at the later trial of Frederick Morse. What we know for certain is that, late in the afternoon, Morse's brother found Frederick wet and weeping. Distraught, Frederick told his brother how he had earlier left Doris in a shed near the River Rag. He had then gone about his business, fetching a number of rabbit traps. On his return, the girl had gone and he had spent the remainder of his time searching the fields and woods and along the river bank. In so doing he had himself fallen into the river. The river can be cold at the best of times, but this was February, and there he sat shivering and weeping.

No trace could be found of the girl until the discovery of her body in the river the following day. The post mortem, which inevitably followed, revealed that she had drunk a quantity of rum shortly before drowning.

The prosecution argued successfully that she had been murdered; that her uncle, in order to resolve the problem of his pregnant niece, either caused her to be drunk in order to drown her, or came up with some sort of suicide pact into which they both entered, although he had no intention of making the same journey to the other side. When the girl was in a sufficiently drunken state, he had simply pushed her into the river.

On 8th March 1933, the trial for the murder of young Doris opened. The jury favoured the prosecution's case, and on 24th July of that year, Pierrepoint, England's last official executioner, carried out the death by hanging of Frederick Morse at Horfield Prison in Bristol.

The rape and murder of Sarah Watts

Sarah Watts was a happy child, living life much as any other 14 year old girl in her home village of West Woodlands, just two miles from Frome, in the beautiful countryside bordering the Longleat estate. Her parents, John and Leah Watts, occupied a dairy farm and on the morning of Wednesday, 24th September 1851, set out for Frome, as was their regular practice, to sell their wares at the town's market. Sarah had reached an age where she would share the farm chores and hence was accustomed to being left at home on such occasions. But this tragic day was not to be like any other. Indeed it was to be Sarah's last.

Imagine the shock of the parents on arriving home at four in the afternoon. The first indication that all was not well was when there was no answer from Sarah to their calls of 'We're home'. But the dawning of realisation commenced when John Watts spotted blood on the kitchen floor. Calling again for his daughter, John went through to the adjoining dairy. One of their dogs was lapping blood from the floor, where the poor girl lay, clothes torn, body battered and bruised, and quite dead. The surgeon's report prepared for the inquest revealed that Sarah had been raped and shockingly abused before being suffocated by strangulation.

Devastated, John picked up the limp and bloody body of his daughter and carried her upstairs. The local police were notified and the investigation into the circumstances around Sarah's murder began. The following Monday, a detective called Smith, appointed by the Home Office, was put in charge of the case. Although the murder was now five days old, he set about his task in a most professional and thorough way. The facts began to unfold.

At the time of the murder, some bread, butter and cheese had disappeared, perhaps suggesting an opportunist robbery gone badly wrong. A room upstairs had been ransacked, and clothes and a watch had been taken. On the kitchen table lay a silk handkerchief which belonged to no member of the family. The detective made further discoveries. Examining the blood on the dairy floor, he also observed spilt whey. Examination of the whey tub indicated some presence of blood. When the tub was emptied, more blood was found at its bottom. On the dairy door was a handprint with blood on the thumb. A shoe mark on the wall matched a scuff mark on the shoe of the victim and her clothes appeared to have spent some time in the whey tub.

Amazingly, no neighbours or passers-by had seen or heard anything unusual, but then the house was about a hundred yards from the road. Sarah had last been seen by a neighbour at about one o'clock. So who could have committed the ravaging of this young girl?

Further questions from the detective amongst the community, seeking answers as to the whereabouts of each and every person during the course of that afternoon, revealed that three men, each of whom lived in the area, Robert Hurd, William Sparrow and William Maggs, had all been drinking together in a public house at the time that Sarah's parents were passing on their way to market. Sparrow knew the family reasonably well and knew the routine which took Sarah's parents to the market. He would have been aware of the expected time of their return and the fact that young Sarah was now at home alone. At about midday, the three were overheard making arrangements to meet in about an hour and then they went their separate ways.

Around two o'clock, they were seen not far from, and heading in the direction of, the Watts' family home. Hurd was in the lead and encouraging the other two on but they were then seen without him. Around three o'clock, a man was spotted running away from the scene of the crime. Between then and the discovery of the body, they were seen again but now all in different clothes and Maggs was seen passing something on to Hurd.

Later in the afternoon they were also all seen in the market place at Frome and one of them was heard to mention '... a watch but no tin', as if referring to having found a watch but no money.

The evidence was mounting. Three other witnesses testified that the handkerchief left on the kitchen table belonged to Sparrow, although he denied having had a handkerchief for at least seven years.

Perhaps the real giveaway came at North Bradley Fair. On Monday 29th September, the very day the detective started his investigation, Sparrow was talking to a Mrs Watson at the fair. Realising he was from Frome, she asked if he had heard of the dreadful murder. He told her of what he was aware, that the child was lying near the whey tub with her dress up over her head, and that she had blows to the head inflicted by a stick, and how she had been in the whey tub and how it had been covered with blood from her head. What was amazing about this declaration was that, at the time of its telling, the detective had yet to uncover these facts and they had yet to be revealed to the public. Only someone involved with the crime could have been aware of such details. The lady continued by asking if he knew how it had been done and he described how Sarah had been hit with a stick and was held in the whey tub until dead and then put on the floor.

Around the same time, Maggs was in conversation with a person unrelated to the crime. Their conversation had in part been overheard. Maggs was heard to say that he believed that Sparrow was going to 'peach', to 'split on his colleagues' in modern parlance, and would thereby gain a pardon and possibly be able to claim a £50 reward. Maggs pointed out that Sparrow could not do that, since he was the one who had killed the girl when she had recognised him. Further evidence gathered by the detective suggested that Hurd was the brains behind the robbery but beyond the planning stage only acted as an accomplice.

The following day, the Tuesday, Sparrow was arrested on account of a watch in his possession, which was assumed to be the one taken from the house. He claimed he had bought it from Hurd in the presence of Maggs and this led to the arrest of all three. As it happened, no owner for the watch was ever found but its existence was sufficient to allow the officer to effect the arrests. Sparrow was further questioned by the detective, who noticed Sparrow's hand was bandaged. Asked how he had injured his hand, Sparrow explained that it had been bitten in a row the previous day, but closer examination showed the wound to be festering and clearly dating back to a few days before. A day later, Sparrow was arrested on another charge.

The trial of the three men commenced on 8th April 1852 and no fewer than forty-three witnesses were called. At nine o'clock in the evening of the first day, the prosecution completed the presentation of its evidence and the court retired until the following morning. The defence solicitor then took up the case, claiming that never had he previously seen a prosecution with such a flimsy base. The watch that had led to the arrest of the three men was not the one stolen from the house. There was no evidence that it had been obtained in anything other than a legal manner. The remainder of the evidence against the men was circumstantial and not enough 'to hang a dog'.

It appears that it was the defence case which prevailed. This is amazing, at least in the case of Sparrow. Had he not virtually confessed at North Bradley Fair by revealing details which at that time could only have been known by the killer? Had he not been seen in the right place at the right time? Did he not have an unexplained bite mark on his hand, and was it not his handkerchief on the kitchen table? Sparrow was lucky indeed to escape the hangman's noose.

METEORS AT WESTONZOYLAND

———————— ✿ ————————

I was wandering around the village of Westonzoyland and popped into the old cemetery across the road from that wonderful Somerset church in which so many rebels were held after the Monmouth Rebellion. War graves always stand out, white and proud, from the lichen-covered, neglected remainder. I passed one from the First World War, then another, and then came to thirteen pristine headstones grouped together in two neat rows, each with the winged motif of the RAF. What could have caused so many RAF deaths in one village?

The engravings on the headstones were as follows:

Pilot Officer S.B. Frankel	7 November 1952	age 19
Pilot Officer R.K. Woods	9 February 1953	age 20
Sergeant F.J.S. Stockley	9 February 1953	age 23
Wing Commander J.A. Roncoroni, DFC	19 March 1953	age 38
Squadron Leader W.F. Hoffman, AFC	28 August 1953	age 39
Pilot Officer I.D.G. Somerside	8 September 1953	age 21
Pilot Officer R.M. Bent	14 October 1953	age 24
Pilot Officer F.E. Fry	12 February 1954	age 26
Pilot Officer R.J. Tilley	12 February 1954	age 24
Pilot Officer D.H. Butterworth	19 November 1954	age 24
Flight Lieutenant J.W. Wills	10 January 1955	age 24
Flight Lieutenant A.T. Kenworth	10 January 1955	age 27
Flight Lieutenant I. Hastings	2 February 1955	age 32

These were all too late for the Second World War and the wrong time for the Suez crisis and the Korean War. And surely young pilots killed in action would be buried all over the place and not concentrated in one graveyard? And these pilots weren't all killed at the same time. It was as if every couple of months there was some sort of accident or mishap. The answer lay in part in various copies of the local paper, the *Bridgwater Mercury*. In its pages I discovered that the unlucky number did not stop at thirteen. I found other reports of the deaths or disappearance of flying officers which revealed three more deaths. I carried out research at the RAF Museum at Hendon, where I found the internal enquiry reports, which produced another two pilots killed in the same incidents as those I was investigating. The number of young pilots killed in a period of twenty-seven months totalled eighteen. To the above list, I was able to add:

Flying Officer
  Tony Ronald Valen Evans   7 November 1952
Pilot Officer J.R. Shaw   11 March 1953
Flight Lieutenant R.W. Pinder   16 March 1954
Pilot Officer M.N. Huggins   16 March 1954
Flying Officer J.H. Marvin   2 February 1955

I now realise that there were at least as many unreported deaths as those reported, and those killed were not necessarily buried at Westonzoyland. On that basis it is reasonable to assume that the total number of young pilots lost is in excess of twenty and probably approaching thirty and all the deaths were from one aerodrome. On average during that period, a pilot was killed every four to six weeks. How on earth could that have been allowed to happen? All flying accidents must come down to one of three root causes: pilot error, aircraft failure or act of God. Perhaps some background to the mystery is required.

It was during the Second World War that Sir Frank Whittle developed the jet engine, and before the war was over the Gloster Aircraft Company had produced the Meteor Mark I as a single seater fighter, which made a successful debut in the closing months of the war. Development started in 1940, at the height of the Battle of Britain, but it was much later before 616 Squadron was to receive the first of its new jet fighters. Initially they were used to shoot down flying bombs and to train pilots in the new techniques required. As the war was coming to an end, the

Meteor had developed to the Mark III version. These planes had a range of over one thousand miles, an air speed in excess of four hundred miles an hour and could climb at over thirty-six feet per second.

Over the years, further variants were produced which bring us to the Meteor Mark VII and back to our airbase at Westonzoyland. The Mark VII was developed as an unarmed trainer aircraft with dual controls. It was used when retraining pilots more familiar with piston driven engines. There was obviously a considerable number of pilots to go through the conversion to jets, but, even allowing for that, at least eighteen deaths in twenty-seven months begs the question: 'What was going on at Westonzoyland aerodrome?

November 1952 – numbers 1 and 2

On 7th November 1952, a Meteor jet from the Westonzoyland aerodrome had just completed a training flight and had come in to land. A mechanic carried out a check of the airframe and the aircraft was refuelled. It was declared ready for take off, and 19 year old Pilot Officer Samuel Bunce Frankel climbed into the front cockpit seat whilst 23 year old Tony Ronald Valen Evans occupied the rear seat. The two pilots took off for what was planned to be a thirty minute flight. A few minutes later Evans called the base, completing his radio check. All was well. That was the last that was heard from the crew.

Over at West Lydford, John Parham, a farm worker, heard the aircraft coming towards him. 'I looked up and it seemed to be flying level,' he told the inquest into the crash. The plane then rolled and went into a spin and disappeared behind a building where it crashed. Lionel Hatcher, a farmer, described how he had heard the plane approaching but it didn't sound quite right. He looked up to see it nose diving to the ground, where it immediately burst into flames. Both pilots died instantly from multiple injuries. An embroidered white glove belonging to Evans was the only aid to the identification of the severely burnt bodies.

Pilot Officer Frankel was buried in the village graveyard at Westonzoyland, with full military honours: the coffin draped in the union flag, a volley fired over the grave and the Last Post played. The coroner, declaring death by misadventure, announced that the cause of the crash was down to the RAF to decide.

February 1953 – numbers 3 and 4

On 9th February 1953, Pilot Officer Raymond Kenneth Woods and Sergeant Frederick James Samuel Stockley, who had recently married, took off on a training flight over Exmoor. It was an exciting time for Woods as he approached the end of his National Service and was soon to go to Cambridge University, an ambition he was not to fulfil.

As in the previous case, it was not the first flight that morning and there were no apparent problems with the aircraft. But somewhere near Tarr Steps it crashed. One eye-witness described how the plane had come out of the clouds upside down; another described it flying on its side clipping the tree tops before it crashed. Woods' body was found half a mile from the plane. His parachute was unopened and still in its pack. Stockley was found in Westwater Wood, a full mile away and his parachute had clearly been deployed; the cords were attached to the harness but no parachute was found. It appears he was attempting to bale out but too late.

The coroner's opinion was that the cause of the crash was probably pilot error. He told those present that the accident was not related to the mechanics of the jet plane, as he had been reassured that there were no more accidents with the jet planes than there had been before the war with the piston type machines. He may have been speaking prematurely! The RAF's internal enquiry report shows that these two pilots had over five hundred flying hours' experience between them. It also indicated that the icing index, which measures the likelihood of parts of the plane icing up, was high and that this probably caused certain instrumentation to malfunction, including the altimeter. It emphasised the importance of the early supply of certain newly developed parts.

March to August 1953 – numbers 5, 6 and 7

On 11th March Pilot Officer J. R. Shaw took off on an evening flight from Westonzoyland. Again, it was a Meteor Mark VII. As his plane passed over Bridgwater, residents noticed how the sound of the engines was not that with which they had become familiar. The first news of there being something amiss came when the Netherlands News Agency in the Hague picked up a ship's radio message. It began to sound as though the aircraft had exploded somewhere over the Bristol Channel and crashed into the sea about three miles off Watchet. Spotting a maroon, the Weston lifeboat crew swung into action. The search continued the following day with ships, flying boats and fellow pilots from Westonzoyland scouring the Channel, hoping to spot a Mae West life jacket, but all to no avail.

On 19th March, Wing Commander J.A. Roncoroni died, aged thirty-eight, and in August Squadron Leader W.F. Hoffman likewise died, aged thirty-nine. There is no evidence that I have found to indicate their cause of death, so it would be unfair to suggest that their untimely ends resulted from Meteor crashes, but they fit into the same period.

The summer produced something of a lull in aircraft crashes, at least reported ones, but there was clearly cause for concern, as shown in the report of a meeting of the Bridgwater Town Council. The members expressed their fears that it was only a matter of time before a Meteor crashed on the town unless instructions were issued to fly around the built-up area.

September and October 1953 – numbers 8 and 9

On 8th September 1953, Pilot Officer Ian Somerside was killed when structural failure occurred in the air at an altitude of around fifteen to twenty thousand feet. This was followed by a fire in the fuselage. The aircraft spiralled downwards, parts falling off as it descended. The internal investigation suggested the root cause was the high negative G force. The medical report suggested that loss of consciousness of the pilot occurred due to the inhalation of fuel. Could this also have been what had happened to the earlier pilots? Had their aircraft suffered structural failure? Had fuel fumes caused unconsciousness, resulting in flying upside down?

Pilot Officer Ronald Mills Bent had been briefed for aerobatic manoeuvres prior to his flight on 14th October 1953. His aircraft had been serviced every three days. He was an above average pilot and had carried out aerobatic manoeuvres several times before. There was nothing to suggest a forthcoming disaster, but somewhere out over the Bristol Channel something went terribly wrong. Back in the control tower they received a message from Bent stating he was in an inverted spin at ten thousand feet. The message was followed immediately by a May Day call. Nothing more was heard from the pilot.

The aircraft was never found, but Bent's body turned up in the estuary of the River Parrett some two weeks later. His face had suffered serious injuries, suggesting it had smashed violently forwards and upwards into the cockpit window on hitting the water. The pilot had been disconnected from his parachute and safety harness, which indicated that he knew he would be landing in the water. At the inquest the coroner stated that the cause of death was a broken spine and emphasised that death was not caused because it was a jet engine aircraft. This was an unexpected comment from the coroner, when at previous inquests the coroners had stated it was not for them to speculate on the cause of the accident – that was the role of the RAF. It was almost as if there was a conspiracy to hush up what was going on in respect of the Meteor Mark VIIs.

February and March 1954 – numbers 10, 11, 12 and 13

February 12th saw the loss of two aircraft and two pilots. Pilot Officers R. J. Tilley and F. E. Fry had both taken off on a night flight along with other aircraft. Unfortunately, while they were airborne, another aircraft had landed with its undercarriage up and was now blocking the runway. The young officers were diverted to Merryfield, where the low cloud was causing problems, making the landing strip almost impossible to find. Whether their altimeters were working or not is not detailed in the reports, but, whatever the cause, the two pilots independently of each other simply flew into the ground. One crashed just a hundred yards from Thickthorn Manor on the Taunton to Ilminster road. The wreckage was strewn over three fields. The other came down at Barrington.

Just four weeks later, on 16th March, the Bridgwater Mercury reported that appeals were being made for two airmen missing

RAF graves at Westonzoyland

from Westonzoyland. BBC news bulletins broadcast the news of the disappearing Meteor in which Flight Lieutenant R. W. Pinder and his pupil Pilot Officer M. N. Huggins had taken off on a routine training flight. No radio message was ever received from either pilot. The ships in the Bristol Channel were requested to keep a watchful eye for signs of wreckage. Fellow airmen from the base flew reconnaissance flights over the channel. Neither plane nor pilots were found.

Once again, through the summer months all goes quiet except for a couple of Vampires crashing on Exmoor.

November 1954 – number 14

On 19th November 1954, Flying Officer D. H. Butterworth was on exercise over the Bristol Channel. For some unknown reason his navigation equipment failed to function. Assistance was sought from the aerodromes at Chivenor and Merryfield, which tried to give him instructions. It was soon realised that he was actually heading in the wrong direction. Advised to find the coastline and follow it, he did just that but then had to bale out as his fuel ran out. His body was recovered some hours later. The RAF internal enquiry suggested that the remedial action for this type of incident was to provide pilots with dinghies! This suggests that solutions were addressing the symptoms and not the cause. By this point in my research I had a very positive sense of an organisational unpreparedness to take a close look at the real cause of the loss of so many aircraft and lives.

10th January 1955 – numbers 15 and 16

It was a morning of light misty rain when Flight Lieutenant John William Wills of The Cottage, Holway Green in Taunton and his co-pilot, Flight Lieutenant Alexander Telford Kenworth, whose home was in Lincolnshire, took off on a routine flight. These were both pilots with considerable experience. Wills had joined the RAF in 1949 and was now an instructor. Flight Sergeant Wilfred Blewett who was in charge of servicing the plane had given it the all clear in all respects although a fuel tank had recently been replaced. From the control tower, traffic control watched as the jet taxied to the runway, increased in speed and began its ascent. They watched as it flew off, heading across the nearby river. A message was received, indicating the pilots' intention to head towards Yeovilton. Just four minutes into the flight, disaster struck.

Mrs W. Coombes of Drysend Farm and Mrs Greenacre of 2, Sunny View were busy doing their washing in the normally quiet village of Moorland, just across the River Parrett from the area surrounding the Westonzoyland airfield. They could hear the sound of a Meteor Mark VII jet approaching and coming in quite low through the mist. Then they heard a loud explosion while the plane was still in the air. Then they saw dense smoke and flames running along the ground.

The two ladies dropped their chores and immediately ran across the fields towards the disaster area, jumping the rhynes as they did so. What they found were bits of plane and parts of bodies scattered all over the area; indeed, debris was spread over a mile radius. As this was not an easy place to access, the ladies were well ahead of anyone else arriving at the scene and were then followed by a nearby farmer. He also had seen the incident and at the inquest stated how he took little notice of the plane at first. Seeing jets in this area was very common. There was nothing unusual in its behaviour to draw his attention. But then he saw it burst into flames and was sure this was before it crashed.

It was a full half hour before the RAF, police and fire brigade began to arrive. As they approached the scene, there before them were the two gallant ladies wading towards them, knee deep in mud. Identification of the pilots' bodies was only possible by documentation in their clothing.

2nd February 1955 – numbers 17 and 18

Flight Lieutenant Ian Hastings was living locally at The Mount on Berrow Road in Burnham-on-Sea. He was joined by John Harold Marvin of Durleigh Road, Bridgwater for the fateful flight on 2nd February. Both men were at the Westonzoyland airbase as pilot instructors. Hastings had been in the service since 1941 and had been an instructor for two and a half years. Marvin had been an instructor for three months. Although one had considerably more experience than the other, they were both nonetheless very experienced pilots and as such were at the base for continuation training, which took place every month.

It was 8.14 am when they prepared for take off and permission to do so was given by the control tower. Weather conditions were perfect with little or no cloud, just bright sunlight. Only the previous day the plane in which they flew had been tested and was described as behaving perfectly. The jet had dual controls and so it was impossible after the event to determine who had been in control at the time. In the air simultaneously was Squadron Leader Franklin, who heard one of the two pilots, just six minutes after take off, request permission to enter a low flying area near Durston. At the local inquest it was revealed that no one after the event could remember permission being granted although that would not appear to have had any effect on the tragic outcome of this flight. However, the report from the internal enquiry indicated that permission was given. Why should the evidence be contradictory between the two enquiries?

Just one minute after that request to enter the low fly zone was made, a large plume of smoke rose from an orchard in the fields near the village of Durston. A shed in the orchard had been demolished and amazingly the turkeys within all survived – but not so the pilots. Squadron Leader Franklin flew in closer to investigate. A Williton policeman by chance was driving about two miles away and headed towards the plume of smoke. He described how he had seen the plane climbing slightly until the nose dipped violently and it went into a steep dive. The plane then cut through overhead wires, hit a workshop, destroyed a motorcycle and crashed.

Doris Trott, living at Lower Durston, heard the plane approaching behind her house at about three quarters throttle and climbing. The engine then appeared to go quiet, the jet banked onto its left wing and went straight into an uncontrolled dive to terra firma.

At the inquest, the coroner remarked it was unlikely the cause of the accident would ever be known and that it was down to the RAF to carry out internally whatever investigations were appropriate. Was that the right attitude at the inquest into yet another fatal crash? Wasn't a public enquiry appropriate? Was there pressure from the RAF or MOD to suppress any public debate? These were the years not long after the war, when it was in the culture of the nation to play down any bad news and suppress any criticism of the armed services.

At the internal enquiry, it was reported that the aircraft had been seen flying through a series of badly executed manoeuvres. It was suggested that the captain, who was in the front seat, was probably affected by fatigue and the after effects of the previous night's drinking.

The aftermath

What had been the real cause of these tragic events? Was pilot error to blame? We can see that most of the pilots had considerable experience. In some cases they were pilots who were deemed to be sufficiently experienced to be given the responsibility for training others. Was it mechanical failure, or perhaps metal fatigue? Was it appropriate to allow such training to continue, at least until an enquiry had been set up to establish the root cause of this catalogue of tragedies?

In April 1955 the *Bridgwater Mercury* announced that the jet aircraft training school at the air station at Westonzoyland was to be taken over, to be replaced by RAF Bomber Command. The training school would close, leaving behind thirteen graves in the nearby village cemetery and many others elsewhere. The report continued as follows: 'At the last parish meeting at Westonzoyland it was stated that the RAF was not making any more requests for use at the cemetery.' But it all came too late for the Meteor pilots of this unhappy time.

A POLITICALLY MOTIVATED KILLING

———————— ❀ ————————

Ted Lethaby was an AA patrolman and quite used to the unexpected – but on 24th October 1975 he came across a situation which was to hit the international headlines and trigger a major political scandal. It was around 9 o'clock in the evening and it had already been dark some three hours. Ted was driving east towards Porlock along the scenic coast road, with the lights of South Wales visible across the Bristol Channel. As he approached the Yenworthy Lodge Farm turning, he saw in his headlights a man in the middle of the road waving his arms for Ted to stop. He pulled in. But this was nothing like any routine stop for the AA man, for there at the roadside lay the warm but dead body of a big black Great Dane, with a bullet hole in its head.

The Great Dane, Rinka, had been the pet of 35 year old former male model Norman Scott of Combe Martin, who now stood, frightened and hysterical, as he blurted out his story. An attempt had just been made to kill him, he claimed. Its purpose was to ensure that what he knew about the Right Honourable Jeremy Thorpe, the MP for North Devon, should never be published. Jeremy Thorpe at the time was also a Privy Councillor and leader of the Liberal Party.

Very soon a road block had been set up around the area. The police were seeking airline pilot Andrew Gino Newton, the driver of a Ford Escort car, with whom Norman Scott had driven to that fateful spot, but already he had slipped the net.

Earlier that evening, Scott and Newton had met at the Castle Hotel in Porlock. Some months before, Newton had befriended Scott and became a self-appointed protector to the other man, who had said that he feared for his personal safety. At least that was Newton's cover story, but it appears the friendship may have been struck up for other purposes. Whatever the reason, on the journey back to Devon, they had stopped, got out of the car and there Newton had shot Scott's dog. According to Scott, Newton then declared, 'Now it's your turn,' but when he pulled the trigger, the gun jammed and Scott was spared. Newton drove off, leaving Scott to grieve over the loss of his dog and to wonder what might have been had the gun not jammed – and also to wonder if Newton would return to finish the job.

But what was the background that led to this strange affair? In a number of subsequent court cases the story was to unfold, much of which had its roots just across the border in North Devon.

It was in October 1959 that the Conservative Party was returned to power with a thumping majority and many new MPs were to join the Westminster establishment. One new face was that of Margaret Thatcher. Another new face for the Liberals was the former Oxford Union president Jeremy Thorpe who had just been elected as the Member of Parliament for the North Devon constituency. It had been a disastrous election for the Liberals as they had only gained six per cent of the poll and hence any Liberal victory was to be applauded. In the years that followed Jeremy Thorpe was to become a popular, much respected and hard working representative for his constituency and played an increasingly high profile role within his party. He proved to be an eloquent speaker in the House. On one occasion in July 1962, shortly after a huge Liberal success at a by-election, the Conservative Prime Minister within a twenty-four hour period sacked seven members of his cabinet. Jeremy Thorpe quipped, 'Greater love hath no man than this, that he lays down his friends for his life.' Here was a man to be noticed and in January 1967, in the wake of the resignation of Jo Grimond, the thirty-seven year old extrovert Old Etonian Jeremy Thorpe was elected to lead his party. In 1968 he married his first wife, Caroline Allpass, who died in a car crash not long after the birth of their son, and later, in 1973, he married the Countess of Harewood.

But during those early years, so Mr Peter Taylor QC alleged many years later at a much publicised Old Bailey trial, a character by the name of Norman Scott had a homosexual relationship with Thorpe and thereafter Scott remained a risk to the political advancement of Thorpe, not least because Scott spoke fairly openly of the relationship and actually moved into the North

Devon constituency and boasted in public houses about how he would reveal all in a book. This could spell political disaster, whether true or not, for any MP, and Britain was entering a critical political phase.

The winter of 1973/74 had seen the miners' strike and a winter of discontent. Prime Minister Edward Heath went to the nation with a general election on the basis of who runs the country, parliament or the miners? The result of the election was a hung parliament with neither Labour nor Conservatives having an overall majority. A government could only be formed by a coalition, by either party, with the Liberals. Jeremy Thorpe and his fellow MPs held the key to power. The Liberal share of the vote under Thorpe's leadership had increased to twenty-four per cent. Labour under Harold Wilson formed a minority government and could only pray that he could make it work. He would depend heavily on the support of the Liberals throughout that period. By October of that year, a general election had been forced on the minority government, and Labour was this time returned with a small overall majority. It was a campaign during which Jeremy Thorpe, as extrovert as ever, used a hovercraft to get himself around – unfortunately it crashed!

Rumours of Jeremy Thorpe's alleged homosexual activities had been doing the rounds for some while, but the press were unable to openly speculate for fear of prosecution. But then came their opportunity on 16th March 1976, some months after the shooting incident, when Norman Scott was in court at an industrial tribunal during which he openly made reference to Jeremy Thorpe and their 'live-in' relationship. The story was to break to the public for the first time. Coincidentally, in the same month at another trial, Andrew Newton, who for a while had left the country but was arrested on his return, was facing charges of possessing a firearm with intent to endanger life. He initially denied the charges but later admitted to perjury, was convicted on the firearms charge and sentenced to two years' imprisonment. During the trial he claimed that Scott had a nude photo of him and was using it to blackmail him. The shooting incident, he claimed, was to terrify Scott into returning the picture.

Within weeks, Jeremy Thorpe, unable to withstand what he called 'a sustained press witch-hunt and campaign of denigration', had resigned as leader of his party. 'No man can effectively lead a party if the greater part of his time has to be devoted to answering allegations and countering plots and intrigues,' he argued. Just two days later, Harold Wilson, who had recently himself unexpectedly resigned as Prime Minister, called on two journalists to expose a South African plot to discredit Jeremy Thorpe. The plot was thickening.

Meanwhile, the allegations made by Scott of an attempt on his life were being investigated by the Department of Public Prosecutions. A detective chief superintendent from the Avon and Somerset Constabulary flew to the United States to interview Peter Bessell, a close friend of Jeremy Thorpe, who had previously been the Liberal MP for Bodmin. The impact of that interview was startling, and as a result Jeremy Thorpe was charged with conspiracy to murder Norman Scott and Bessell became a key witness for the prosecution at the ensuing trial. Accused along with Thorpe were fellow Liberal David Holmes, John Le Mesurier, a carpet dealer from South Wales, and George Deakin, a club owner also from South Wales. At a later date, just Thorpe was charged with unlawfully inciting David Malcolm Holmes to murder Norman Scott. After a preliminary hearing in Minehead, it was considered there was sufficient evidence for all four to stand trial, which they later did at the Old Bailey, but not until after a short delay to permit a General Election, in which Jeremy Thorpe, not surprisingly, lost his seat to the Conservative candidate.

The prosecution's case was that Scott had become a political threat to Thorpe and the Liberal Party and that Holmes had become convinced that Scott had to be killed. Holmes knew John Le Mesurier, who in turn knew George Deakin, who in turn recruited Andrew Newton as the required assassin, with a fee of £10,000. Half of that was paid to Newton on his later release from prison, money which Thorpe himself had procured from a Liberal Party benefactor and which passed through various hands to avoid its being traced back to its donor. Newton, the prosecution alleged, had been briefed by both Deakin and Holmes in respect of the assassination.

After the trial, lasting thirty days, the prosecution case came to a close. The defence readily admitted to an attempt to frighten Scott, but the accusation of conspiracy to murder was vehemently denied. The trial ended on 22nd June 1979, after fifty-two hours of deliberation by the jury, with all four accused deemed 'Not Guilty'.

But the mystery remains. After the shooting of the dog, did the gun really jam or was it all a bluff? Had this been a bungled assassination attempt or simply the intimidation of a blackmailer? Had there been a politically motivated plot to murder Scott? Only Andrew Newton knows for certain the answer to all these questions.

MURDER ON CHILLINGTON COMMON

---⬡---

S imeon Stuckey was a well known and respected builder who was born in Over Stratton near South Petherton. It was there that his aged parents still lived, whilst Simeon had settled in Chard. He was successful in trade, with a number of commercial interests. He owned a farm and in addition had a building business with no fewer than thirty employees. It was high summer in South Somerset in August 1830 and some of those employees were building a new home for his lifelong friend Benjamin Hebditch in Simeon's old village of Over Stratton. Simeon decided to pop over and check that everything was going to his expectations. It was a distance of about ten miles between his home and where his employees were working.

It was already late on that Monday afternoon when he set out and he was undoubtedly quite hot. Along the road from Chard to Crewkerne was the Windwhistle Inn, conveniently about halfway to his destination. Lawrence Biss, the landlord, was a likeable soul and well known to Mr Stuckey, but who knows what shady characters may have lurked in the inn that day.

The Windwhistle can be found today on the A30, which for centuries has been an important road between London and the West Country. In the 17th and 18th centuries it was infamous for the activities of highwaymen, who would lie in wait in the wooded areas at the summit of the hill along this lonely stretch of road. There the traveller's coach would arrive with exhausted horses, no energy left to gallop away. It made easy pickings for those lying in wait. The favourite haunt in which they took shelter and spent their ill-gotten gains was the Windwhistle Inn. Local legend has it that no stranger with money could enter its doors and leave it alive. But far more likely is the fact that strangers who entered and displayed a fat purse would be an obvious soft target

The Windwhistle Inn

for the villains within, who would observe every important detail of each traveller passing through.

Smugglers were also active in these parts, and the nearby villages, including Chillington just along the road from the inn, were reputed to be 'staging points' where smuggled goods coming up from the Dorset coast would be hidden on their way to Bath. But our story is in the less violent days of the 19th century and so we return to Simeon Stuckey, sitting comfortably on a settle as he drank his pint of cider in the Windwhistle Inn and chatted with the friendly landlord. He was not there long and on leaving at about 5.30 pm said to the landlord that he'd see him later, as he'd stop in again on his return journey later that night.

But also in the inn, and surely able to overhear his conversation, there were several others. Among them was a man named Rowe from Winsham, Mr Baker and Joseph Cranton from Cricket St Thomas, Richard Hutchings of Purtington, John, Samuel and William Balford from Butleigh, and Hugh Clarke from the nearby village of Cudworth. Hugh was to tell the later inquest about how he had noticed Simeon Stuckey's bulging purse, made of yellow canvas and looking as though it was full of money. He also saw Simeon leave on his own, and shortly after the landlord's wife came in followed by a stranger in a short smock. There were five or six others as well and any of these could have seen the bulging purse or heard about it in conversation after Simeon had left. Was robbery the motive for what was yet to happen?

Simeon's journey took him through the villages of Chillington and Dinnington, along the Fosse Way to Lopen and Over Stratton. There, at his home village, he visited the building site and then called on his old friend to let him know that all was going well with his new home. At about 10 o'clock in the evening he left Benjamin's house and called briefly on his father, who was laid up ill in bed. The hour already being late, and darkness having fallen, he apologised for the briefness of the visit but promised to call again within a few days.

He commenced his journey home, which was to take him back by Lopen, through Dinnington and onwards to Chillington, a village which he was never to reach alive. It seems that also on that route that night were two strangers to the area. Perhaps they were amongst the several men in the Windwhistle Inn earlier that evening. Whoever they were, one enquired of a local as to whether or not he had seen a man dressed in the same way as Simeon. The other was seeking directions to Chard and had asked one Margaret Lucy if she was prepared to show him the way. Margaret felt most uncomfortable about the way the question was asked and bolted herself into her cottage.

At about 11 o'clock that evening, a labourer, Robert Perry, who lived in a cottage with his daughter Amy on the road along which Simeon was expecting to travel, heard the sound of a horse galloping past in the direction in which Simeon would pass and in which it was later discovered he had been brutally murdered.

Sometime in the next hour or so, Sheriff's Officer Norris from Crewkerne found a horse wandering on Chillington Common, near the Windwhistle turnpike gate. The horse was now cold but dried sweat marks indicated it had been running hard since it was last saddled up. Being quite close to the Windwhistle Inn, Norris headed off to find Lawrence Biss. It was 1 o'clock in the morning when he stood outside the inn calling for the landlord. Mrs Biss was first to wake and go to the window to see what all the fuss was about so late at night. Norris told her that he had urgent business with her husband. Lawrence Biss shook off the blankets, lit a lantern and went down to see what would bring the sheriff's officer to his door at this hour.

Norris showed him the horse he had found and asked if he recognised it and perhaps could give a clue as to its owner. There was no difficulty at all – it was Simeon Stuckey's horse, Old Tom. In the lantern light, they could see there were no clues as to why it should be unattended. The bridle and saddle were in perfect position. Everything appeared in correct order – apart from the dried sweat marks.

It was agreed that the horse should be kept at the inn, pending its collection by the owner, and the officer, who was returning to Chard, agreed to notify Mrs Stuckey in the morning as to the whereabouts of her husband's horse. Biss unsaddled the horse and turned it out into the field for the night.

Early the following morning, Tuesday, Robert Perry was already on his way to work by 5.30 am, heading towards Dinnington, the direction in which he had heard the horse galloping the previous night. He had gone no more than a hundred yards when at a field gate he saw what appeared to be the contents of someone's stomach. A similar distance further along and he found a gentleman's hat. Unbeknown to him at the time, it was Simeon Stuckey's. He took the hat back to his daughter with instructions to hand it over if anyone came looking for it.

A few hours later, Susan Matthews, who lived locally, walked the same stretch of road and saw vomit and what appeared to be a large quantity of blood, plus a stick. She also saw marks in the road as though there had been a struggle and drag marks as though someone had been pulling a heavy object across the road.

Meanwhile, over at the Windwhistle Inn, Lawrence Biss had prepared breakfast, cleaned up around the inn and was on his way to the woods where he would be cutting timber for the rest of the morning. Returning to the inn at lunchtime, he was perhaps a little disappointed to see Old Tom still grazing in the field. His disappointment turned to concern when he came back again at tea time and Old Tom was still there. He then arranged for the horse to be saddled and bridled and taken to Mrs Stuckey in Chard.

That evening, one of Mrs Stuckey's lads arrived asking for an explanation of the circumstances which brought Old Tom to be held at the inn. Lawrence Biss explained as much as he knew, including how Simeon was on his way to Over Stratton and had failed to return the previous evening. The young lad headed for Over Stratton to complete his enquiries. These gradually revealed the movements of Simeon Stuckey late on the Monday night and how he had left the village an hour or two before his horse had been discovered alone on the common. It was becoming clear, especially now that the information regarding the hat and stick and the vomit and blood had come to light, that something bad might have happened to Simeon. On the Wednesday morning, the search parties scoured the area around the likely scene of Simeon's disappearance but all to no avail. It was realised that the gold watch he wore plus the purse of money he carried were sufficient temptation for him to be chosen as a target by any likely villains.

Two weeks later and his body had still not been discovered. Rumours began to spread along two opposing lines of thought; one that he had been foully murdered, the other that he had engineered his own disappearance. There even began a 'tabloid' war between two local papers. The *Taunton Courier* suggested that the mysterious murder of Simeon Stuckey was neither murder nor mystery. They claimed that, for a man who was quick enough to collect every penny that was owed him, he did not carry out the same practice in respect of those to whom he owed money. Indeed, they suggested, he was considerably overdrawn at the bank and there was great concern from his creditors as to whether they would ever see their money. And had he been murdered as close to the cottages as the blood and vomit suggested, the very cottages where they had heard a horse gallop by; surely someone in the cottages would have heard the dastardly deed being executed. Surely the hat and stick had been deliberately left to ensure Stuckey was identified as the victim of this 'staged' murder. Clearly, in the *Taunton Courier*'s opinion, there was good cause to suspect that Simeon Stuckey had done a bunk in order to avoid meeting his obligations to both his bank and his creditors.

The *Western Flying Post*, however, flew to his defence, contradicting each accusation made by the *Courier* and even offering a one hundred pound reward for information leading to the capture and conviction of Simeon Stuckey's killer. It was their version which proved to be correct.

On the last day of August, just a quarter of a mile from the believed scene of the crime, Edmund and Charles Harris were working in a field belonging to Joseph Harris, their father. There amidst the standing corn, in an area where the crop was somewhat flattened, lay what appeared at first to be a fallen scarecrow. A closer examination revealed a fly blown, badly decomposed body, its eyes pecked out by the birds. Despite the gruesome nature of the body's appearance, once the news broke it wasn't long before quite a crowd of onlookers gathered as the coroner and a rapidly rustled up jury of eighteen good men and true arrived to view the scene.

Identification of the body as being that of Simeon was confirmed by his pocket notebook. His coat and buttons were torn as though that had been used to drag his body to the spot. A gouged out line where his spurs dug in confirmed the suspicion. His watch was still attached to the fob chain, and his money appeared to be intact. Robbery perhaps was no longer the motive but it could have been if the killer had panicked once he realised the seriousness of his crime. The surgeon who conducted the post mortem found the cause of death to have been a severe fracture to the skull, sufficient for death to be instantaneous and to cause the stomach contents to be ejected. There was no way Simeon could have walked from the place of his attack to where his body finally lay.

At the later inquest, a verdict of murder by persons unknown was returned. The suspicion certainly lay with the two strangers who were out on Chillington Common at the very time of the murder, but who they were, no one was ever to discover.

Simeon Stuckey was laid to rest in the grounds of the Independent Church in Chard, where he was a regular attendee. The *Western Flying Post* took great delight in bringing to task the irresponsible reporting of the *Taunton Courier* and calling on them to reveal the sources of their false evidence.

Neither the efforts of Samuel Taunton, a notorious Bow Street Runner, nor the reward money, which was increased to five hundred pounds, proved sufficient to uncover the killer of Simeon Stuckey. This was not the first murder on Windwhistle Hill, not by far, nor was it the last – but those are stories for another time and another place. Meanwhile, the killer of Simeon Stuckey remains a mystery and surely always will.

Acknowledgements

———————— ✿ ————————

David Bromwich, Somerset Studies Library; Lionel McNally; Kathryn Morris; RAF Museum, Hendon; Chris Sidaway.

Bibliography

———————— ✿ ————————

Brewster, Sir David *British Association Report (1855) p9: On the existence of Acari in Mica*

Crosse, Andrew *The American Journal of Science and Arts, Vol 35: p125-137* (January 1839)

Evans, Roger *Bridgwater with and without the 'e'* Roger Evans (1995)

Evans, Roger *Somerset in the Footsteps of Coleridge and Wordsworth* Roger Evans (2000)

Francis, Di *The Beast of Exmoor* Jonathan Cape (1993)

Holt, Alan L. *West Somerset Romantic Routes & Mysterious Byways* Charles Skilton Ltd (1984)

Mead, A. *The story of Fyne Court and Broomfield* Somerset Trust for Nature Conservation (undated)

London Times, 29 and 30 October 1851; 8 and 9 April 1852

Taunton Courier, 18 August through to 15 September 1830

Western Flying Post, 16 August through to 6 September 1830